Mission and the Cultural Other

Mission and the Cultural Other

A Closer Look

RANDY S. WOODLEY
Foreword by BRANDI MILLER

CASCADE *Books* • Eugene, Oregon

MISSION AND THE CULTURAL OTHER
A Closer Look

Copyright © 2022 Randy S. Woodley. All rights reserved. Except for brief quotations in critical publications or reviews, no part of this book may be reproduced in any manner without prior written permission from the publisher. Write: Permissions, Wipf and Stock Publishers, 199 W. 8th Ave., Suite 3, Eugene, OR 97401.

Cascade Books
An Imprint of Wipf and Stock Publishers
199 W. 8th Ave., Suite 3
Eugene, OR 97401

www.wipfandstock.com

PAPERBACK ISBN: 978-1-7252-6385-7
HARDCOVER ISBN: 978-1-7252-6386-4
EBOOK ISBN: 978-1-7252-6387-1

Cataloguing-in-Publication data:

Names: Woodley, Randy S., author | Miller, Brandi, foreword.

Title: Mission and the cultural other : a closer look / by Randy S. Woodley ; foreword by Brandi Miller.

Description: Eugene, OR: Cascade Books, 2022 | Includes bibliographical references.

Identifiers: ISBN 978-1-7252-6385-7 (paperback) | ISBN 978-1-7252-6386-4 (hardcover) | ISBN 978-1-7252-6387-1 (ebook)

Subjects: LCSH: Postcolonial theology | Theology | Indians of North America—Religion

Classification: BT83.593 .W50 2022 (print) | BT83.593 .W50(ebook)

TABLE OF CONTENTS

Foreword by Brandi Miller vii

Introduction: Apparent Contradictions xi

PART 1: *Evaluating the Western Missional Paradigm*

Chapter One: Confessions of a Missionary Oppressor 3

Chapter Two: The Ill-Fated Heathen School Story: Template for Missional Utopianism 12

Chapter Three: Beyond Western Missional Hegemony: The History We Carry 23

Chapter Four: Missional Pedagogy 35

PART 2: *Considering New Missional Foundations*

Chapter Five: Demographic Realities and Whiteness Theologies 49

Chapter Six: Negotiating God's "Four Books" and Questions of Authority 61

Chapter Seven: Human Spirituality without Religion 74

Chapter Eight: Reframing Old Constructs 87

Chapter Nine: Shalom Values and the Humpty Dumpty Dilemma 101

Chapter Ten: The Mission of Jesus 122

Conclusion: Ending at the Beginning 131

Narrative Bibliography 135

Other books by Randy S. Woodley 137

Bibliography 139

Foreword

FOR NEARLY FIFTEEN YEARS, I participated in, and worked for, an evangelical campus ministry. "Mission" was a buzzword meant to encapsulate the grandiose task that God had assigned us to carry out. We built communities of college students, taught them to share the gospel, and invited them to ever increasing purity in their lives. The mission was to see "students and faculty transformed, campuses renewed, world changers developed." On its face, this mission felt harmless and benign at worst, and somehow holy and gallant at best. However, the model was embedded in Western culture and worldviews, and it became clear to me over time that transformation, renewal, and development through the lens of white evangelical Christians, looked much more like spiritual capitalism than it did the community of creation that Jesus invites all beings into.

In our mission model, students were the product of our fundraised money; our numbers and growth were the evidence of God's will and way being manifest in the world through us. In essence, students were objects that we acted upon for the sake of Jesus' great cause. I believe it is by (and I will sound as deeply Christian as I am here) the grace of God that students actually found on-ramps to deeper love for God, self, others, and creation through our work.

As ministers our reality was that *we* carried the great weight of world transformation, as though our minimal salaried role and robust sense of call elevated us more closely to God than the students with whom we interacted. This was *not* the community of creation to which Woodley refers, and rates of burnout, loss of faith, and broken relationships reflected that reality even in the midst of the good things that came from our efforts. Upon reflection, I can see that as we sought to take on the character of Jesus, we more often played the role of God rather than pointing people to

Jesus. We inadvertently shaped the people we "served" into people in our own image. "Follow me as I follow Jesus," we would say.

Many of us in mission have experienced this type of frenetic ministry that increases in intensity as the United States secularizes or rejects this Western iteration of the Jesus Way altogether. The result is that people who see themselves as missionaries or feel called to this type of missional posture feel the need to innovate their lives in such a way that God would be known in the world. This view of God, namely, God as a being who is desperate for our anxious mission work, misses the greater picture of the Creator who loves us and invites us to participate in co-flourishing, rather than the demanding paternalistic laboring for an abstracted heavenly good later.

As I have spent time with Randy and Edith Woodley, and their family, at Eloheh Indigenous Center for Earth Justice, I have come to learn of the Creator who expects us only to be human, and for that to be enough. I have experienced the community of creation in action, a space where people matter more than profit or productivity but where work still gets done because we all contribute, are interconnected, and care.

On one occasion, a group of leaders from our organization arrived at Eloheh to learn from Randy and Edith over a week. Eager to learn new models that would help us reach more students and grow our ministries, we crowded into the Woodleys' living room. There we sat, waiting for a profound teaching to change us, and thus, change the world. Instead, Randy asked each person, one by one, to share their name, the place and people they come from, and something vulnerable about themselves.

As person after person shared, my former mission-mindedness was forced to shift. This wasn't about productivity, knowledge, or mastery, but rather about people being together, grounded in our transparent humanity. It wasn't about competition or performance, but simply about *our* transformation and *our* experience being bound up with one another rather than enshrined in some mythical sense of pure theology or praxis. In this setting, I became aware that what I had been taught prior as a sense of mission was firstly centered on task, responsibility, numbers, and outcomes, but what I was experiencing in the Woodleys' crowded living room at Eloheh was so very different. I was religiously minded but almost entirely lacking the framework that allowed people's well-being to be prioritized above theology, dogma, or notions of purity. And it was, in a word, liberating!

Foreword

My own ministry changed drastically after that trip and I have since been shaped by my friendship with the Woodleys on many subsequent visits. What Randy Woodley presents through his book *Mission and the Cultural Other* offers a window into what I have learned from him in person. It offers space for us to stop and learn from Native Americans, to own the actual guilt we all should feel, if we have a conscience, of American missionary endeavors, and to look to Jesus for a way forward. This book is an invitation away from dutiful, frenetic, and hierarchical missions. The invitation is extended for us all to move forward to a greater pursuit of our place, peace, and community, simply as human participants who are a part of the whole community of creation.

Brandi Miller, *Reclaiming My Theology* **podcast,**
https://www.reclaimingmytheology.com/

Introduction: Apparent Contradictions

I STRUGGLED PERSONALLY WITH whether this book should be written. Granted, this statement is an awkward point from which to begin. Native American scholar William Baldridge warns, "When Indians theologize, they must place one foot into the Euro-American culture; and if they are not careful, they will soon have both feet outside their own culture."[1] The dilemma comes from attempting to offer a perspective that represents my own personal decolonial[2] critique while utilizing the framework of colonial mechanisms and structure. In addition, the project relates to Christian mission, which has almost always been the bane of North American Indigenous communities. This book provides me with a great deal of cultural conflict.

The culpabilities of the Western missionary project are well established but the consequences are even more apparent. This book is both a critique of Western missiological hegemony and a redirection of mission as understood from at least one Indigenous perspective. To begin, I offer one simple definition of colonial missions:

> It is a process in which the "savages" of colonialism are ushered, by earnest Protestant evangelists, into the revelation of their own misery, are promised salvation through self-discovery and civilization, and are drawn into a conversation with modern capitalism—only to find themselves enmeshed, willingly or not, in its order of signs and values, interests and passions, wants and needs.[3]

---

1. "Toward a Native American Theology," 228.

2. R. S. Sugirtharajah in his book *Postcolonial Reconfigurations* (2003) points out the necessity of postcolonial expressions in exposing the link between idea and power and their relationship to Western theories and learning. What I mean by postcolonialism in this context is to expose the colonial thinking in the fabric of Native American mission as it relates to Western thinking, pedagogy, and actions.

3. Comaroff and Comaroff, *Of Revelation and Revolution*, xii.

Introduction: Apparent Contradictions

Indigenous Missiology

My doctoral research, which led to a PhD in intercultural studies, was particularly about Native American values. Personal experience dictates that among the values of traditional Indigenous people is a conviction that life should be *lived* communally and *reflected upon*, for the most part, in private. By taking the Western pedagogical path of writing a book, I have already turned aside from some of those traditional Native American values. Discovery, for Indigenous people, is made in the whole of living life, not through creating extrinsic categories foreign to Indigenous cultures from which to ponder and expound. However, this process is common in Western research, which places primary importance upon the written word. Nevertheless, narrative can also be a very powerful medium and is common among Indigenous people, so I ask you to think of this book as story.

Indigenous people tend to value oral cultural practices over the written word. There remains an Indigenous belief that words have inherent power and especially that they should not be used to deceive others. As is often the case among Indigenous peoples, when words are put into written form, many believe those words lack power because they are without context and taken from outside the vision and *heart* of the speaker. Ronald Niezen, in his book *Spirit Wars*, states,

> There is a tension between written forms of experience and the persistence of oral and nonverbal expression in contemporary Native spirituality. If the spoken word is fraught with unpredictable power, writing can be seen as an even greater source of spiritual compromise.[4]

Native American values teach that each moment is sacred and organic, and recording those sacred moments outside the sacred space from which they took place could be viewed as presumptuous. I will say more about orality later. Indigenous people tend to take life as it comes, giving each moment its due as it occurs. My deepest research concerned itself with Native American values that are ancient and still very deeply rooted among Native Americans and many other Indigenous peoples, especially those who are more traditional and less modern. Regretfully, I must slightly transgress my own cultural values in order to transcend toward examining some of modernity's negative influences upon Native American and other Indigenous people, and perhaps, the whole mission enterprise. I hope my

---

4. Niezen, *Spirit Wars*, 208.

Introduction: Apparent Contradictions

transgression may eventually be forgiven by those who take offense if my efforts can inform others and help to create a better missiology in the future of America's Indigenes and others around the world.

Given the devastating history between Christian mission and Native Americans, my own context, and those of other peoples who have been the object of mission globally, I pose the question of how Christians can attempt to formulate culturally contextual models of mission without repeating the mistakes of the past. In the past, attempts to contextualize missions culturally among American Indians have been hotly contested, especially by Native American Christians who have absorbed Western values.[5] I know the same is true in parts of every continent on the globe. Because of its controversial nature, and for other reasons, deeply cultural contextual mission among Native North Americans and others remains largely ignored by most Western mission agencies and denominations.

Like many people, Indigenous peoples believe that *happiness* and *well-being* are worthwhile goals. Based upon the data, the current state of well-being among Native American people is dire. If Christians are going to continue to do missions among Indigenous peoples, the need for better models is critical.[6] The same is true in foreign mission. In order for better mission models to develop, it makes sense that such models should be based upon those traditional cultural values and not upon the values of the dominant Western society.

Taken as a whole, no standard mission practice is capable of producing an enduring sense of happiness or well-being. This is particularly the case among Native Americans. Two hundred years ago, Tenskwatawa, also known as "the Prophet," and brother to famous Shawnee Indian chief Tecumseh, referenced a sense of happiness or well-being among Native Americans that was in rapid decline. Later, we will take a closer look at the Prophet's words and their relevance for today.

In order for people to find a restored sense of well-being, they need to recover their traditional values and discard the declining and disoriented values of the dominant white society that have been established over the past several centuries. Additionally, there needs to be deep and direct engagement, not through Western culture, but between those cultures and the

---

5. Materials have been produced that are highly critical of contextualization efforts among Native Americans (e.g., Craig Smith, *Boundary Lines*). The critics represent a very conservative evangelical ideological perspective.

6. See Woodley, "Poverty and the Poor."

Introduction: Apparent Contradictions

Scriptures. Through such engagement an overarching theme will surface as a means for producing holistic, culturally sensitive, contextual community-based mission models that are rooted in non-Western values and that produce a sense of well-being for Indigenous and other peoples in the world.

The phenomenon of Indigenous concepts of happiness or well-being are at the forefront of my proposed paradigm. Most often I interpret these concepts through the lens of "harmony" or "balance" in life. Over the years of lived experience and study I have found a set of Indigenous values associated with these concepts of well-being that is shared more broadly among Native Americans and even by other Indigenous people around the world. This way of living and being in harmony often parallels biblical values, and creates a theological foundation for mission. Furthermore, these values draw from a broad-based contextual model of mission among Native North Americans.

In my doctoral research, I set out to explore the possibility that the core values of most Native North Americans might be centered in Indigenous concepts of well-being. For this exploration to occur, I needed to identify the core Indigenous values of various tribes, found within their own well-being concepts, and then attempt to determine whether or not the core Indigenous values could be synthesized easily into one broad conceptuality. I needed to discover whether or not these concepts were more similar or dissimilar to one another before I could attempt to link them to a broad scriptural/theological theme.

Given that Western models of mission have failed miserably among Native Americans and that colonial practices have devastated Native communities, my research sought a better way of pursuing mission among Native Americans. It did so by asking several important preliminary questions: Do Native Americans have a generally shared set of values that could guide the construction of new models for mission in North American Native communities, and, if so, to what degree are these values shared among Native American communities? What resources (particularly values) are available within the Native American communities themselves for developing appropriate models of mission? Could such resources be developed into authentic, integral mission models?

I began the project with a three-pronged framework—from a biblical/theological construction of *shalom*, a contextually based, anthropologically informed missiology, and an Indigenous construction of decolonization and indigenization. A framework for studying values emerged based on

Introduction: Apparent Contradictions

literature from the fields of counseling, sociology, anthropology, education, missiology, history, and religion. The values themselves emerged from conversations with elders/spiritual leaders who participated in extensive interviews. I also surveyed over one hundred Native Americans. All the survey responses and interview responses were analyzed using grounded theory as a way to discover and organize a system of values. I linked responses with literature regarding Native American value studies, discourse, and experiences as the value categories emerged. I was able to establish among Native Americans a widely spread construct I call the "Harmony Way." I was then able to isolate and examine ten commonly held core values that exist within the framework of the Native American Harmony Way, upon which the framework of this book is built.

The research, along with my years of experience both as a missionary and as an anti-missionary, raised questions about current approaches to Native American mission and about the dangers of formulating mission models that are not based on Native American values and not within the framework of a Native American concept of "well-being" or what I will refer to as the "Native American Harmony Way." I hope my research will contribute to the practice of disrupting systems of oppression, especially in the missionary movement, and encourage the formation of alliances to promote Native American models of service that are empowering and liberating for all.

In the Way of Biography and Social Location

My wife and I, with our three youngest children, traveled for nearly four years as a part of our service among Indigenous North Americans. During those four years, we came to realize that we had, to a large degree, a converse mission appointment from Native America back to the dominant white Western culture. We were, if you will, "double agents." By attempting to discover Indigenous context for mission we came to realize that we were the ones who needed the truth and beauty found in Native America as much or more than Native American people needed to hear the truth of the Jesus story. In time, we came to realize both conversions were simultaneously possible. While living in juxtaposition with Christianity and Indigenous spirituality, our experiences bore out the truth that the Western worldview was in dire need of being saved from itself, and healed through America's, and the world's, Host Peoples.

Introduction: Apparent Contradictions

In those four years spent largely on the road, we averaged about sixty thousand miles annually, crisscrossing the country from one place to the next. For example, I remember one week we were attending the Blessing of the Lake Ceremony at the Big Grassy Reserve in Ontario, Canada. And the next week we were dancing at the first church-sponsored Pow Wow in Regina, Saskatchewan. The following week we spent on the Hopi Reservation in Arizona, which included sitting high atop a mesa attending a Bean Dance Ceremony and then the next week I was the emcee at a Pow Wow in Alabama. In between all these places there was invariably a stop or two at a church or university or a seminary where we would share our experiences of the good things that we were learning in all our travels.

Those travels took us all over the United States and Canada, experiencing the richness of so many different cultures, tribally and otherwise. I always liked to have a map for every unknown journey we took (this was before the days of GPS). In the spirit of those years of a missional context, (and in an effort to lay all my cards on the table), I would like to disclose to you, the reader, my particular social location and a few key terms that might help to understand references in this book.

I am a first-generation college-educated male, born in 1956. I have spent most of my career working with people from similar backgrounds to me and the family that raised me; namely, working-class poor people, Indigenous and otherwise (meaning those of us who work for a living but have nothing in a savings account for emergencies) and people who are often the most disenfranchised of society. Ironically, as I am now near the end of my formal career, I have found myself thrown into the sometimes-hostile pit of the erudite world of academia. I use the term "ironically" because I don't come from people whose highest value is education. My family roots are in the Deep South, Alabama and Mississippi to be exact, and also Michigan and Oklahoma.

I was born in Alabama but raised in a blue-collar, multiracial, working poor community called Willow Run, Michigan, located southeast of Detroit. Over time I earned, with some reluctance, a bachelor of arts, a master of divinity, and finally, at age fifty-six, a PhD, in the area of intercultural studies. I am a Cherokee descendant recognized by the United Keetoowah Band of Cherokee Indians in Oklahoma, but since leaving Oklahoma in 2004, and living among various tribal groups, I regretfully have had very little meaningful contact with people from my tribal affiliation. Both my

Introduction: Apparent Contradictions

parents are from mixed-blood Cherokee Indian and white lineage, both fully assimilated into white society.

My father, Ruben, was one of nine children who was raised on a small farm in rural Mississippi. He achieved a twelfth-grade education. He was a World War II Navy veteran who, in response to the bombing of Pearl Harbor, joined the US Navy the day after he graduated high school. My father worked most of his life in a company he started as a carpenter/housebuilder. My dad was ninety-five years old at the time of this writing but has recently passed. My mother, Anne, has an eighth-grade education. As the eldest daughter in a family of ten, it was necessary for her to quit school and move to the city with an aunt in order to work and send money home to her family. She spent most of her career as a beautician. Mom also just passed away at age ninety-three. On my maternal side, I am of the first generation of non-coal miners in three generations. My maternal grandfather was instrumental in establishing the United Mine Workers in central Alabama. My dad's people, regardless of their other professions, like constable, store owner, or minister, were all farmers.

Most of my life of service, missionary and otherwise, has been spent among both traditional and Christian Native American communities, attempting to empower the most neglected people in America. I, and my wife, Edith, an Eastern Shoshone tribal member who grew up on the Wind River Indian Reservation in Wyoming, have four grown children and five grandchildren. Together, we co-sustain an Indigenous, regenerative farm, seed company, spiritual community, and learning center twenty miles southwest of Portland, Oregon called Eloheh Indigenous Center for Earth Justice and Eloheh Farm.

I have founded or cofounded several grassroots organizations over the span of my life, including Cross Cultural Concerns, Christians for Justice, the North American Institute for Indigenous Theological Studies, Evangelicals 4 Justice, the Coalition for Healing Earth and Water, Eagle's Wings Ministry, Eagle Valley Church, and Eloheh Village for Indigenous Leadership—now Eloheh Indigenous Center for Earth Justice and Eloheh Farm and Seeds. I have also served on the boards of several organizations, such as the Portland Area Native American Climate Council and the Oregon Department of Education American Indian/Alaska Native Advisory Council.

I've often referred to myself as a "bridge." At this point it may be helpful to know just a bit more about how I, as a bridge, was built. I don't remember a time when I didn't think of myself as an Indian, although as a young

Introduction: Apparent Contradictions

person I was estranged from any form of a traditional Indian environment. Not coincidentally, I have been involved for many decades among various tribal peoples in what others have dubbed the Native American Contextual Movement, although even my attitudes about that have changed over the past ten or so years.

I have been extremely fortunate, having been exposed to the teachings of elders and spiritual leaders from all three federally recognized Cherokee tribes and from many of those folks who are Cherokee but are not officially recognized as such. In addition, through my life's work and through Indigenous adoptions and friendships I have had the privilege to have varying degrees of familiarity with tribal groups of peoples, including Kiowa, Comanche, various Apache tribes, Wichita, Delaware, Southern Cheyenne, Arapaho, Eastern Shoshone, Choctaw, Creek, Seminole, Shawnee, Ojibway, Crow, Hopi, Navajo, Lakota, Dakota, Washoe, Paiute, Western Shoshone, Confederated Tribes of the Grand Ronde, Yupik, Inuit, and Aleut. I have also spent meaningful times learning from other Indigenes, including Hawaiians, Maori, Samoans, Australian Aboriginals, Maasai, Filipino, and Saami peoples.

One might think that after all this influence, exposure, and thought concerning clashes between the dominant white culture and Indigenous cultures that there is a possibility that I have the right stuff to speak objectively of the American cultural milieu of which I am a part. If that is what you think, you would be wrong. To become your trustworthy guide requires me to be very candid.

Cultural Settings

To begin an honest journey together, I hope, means that we can be honest with ourselves. Therefore, I admit to you that having been a part of both Native American and white Western cultures for so very long, I have a bias *for* Indigenous American cultures and worldviews, and a bias *against* the current Western American culture and worldview. Yet, I do fully live in both cultures and I find things about the dominant American culture and worldview that I like very much. As you may well know to some degree from struggling with your own identity, attempting to sort through culture and worldview issues can be a prickly exercise.

An Indigenous identity process becomes difficult because there really is no *one* Indigenous or even just one Native American culture, any

Introduction: Apparent Contradictions

more than there is *one* American culture. For example, my white, adopted elder brother, Tom, an actual buckaroo who lives on a rural Indian reservation in Nevada, and my good friend Jimmy, who is African American and originally hails from Chicago's South Side (but currently lives in Atlanta), both live in American culture. One spends most of his time surrounded by sagebrush and open sky on a saddle or driving a truck; the other looks around from his vehicle and sees mostly bricks, steel, and blacktop. They live in two distinctly different American cultures and both, incidentally, have Cherokee ancestry.

American Indian cultures can be urban, rural, and suburban. Native American people may be assimilated to a particular dominant white cultural milieu and still continue to be almost totally traditionally Indigenous in their worldview, or perhaps, more likely, they live in various degrees in between. There are elder Indian cultures and youth Indian cultures. Navajo are different than Cherokee; Lakota are different from Kalapuyans, and even within those tribes there are stark differences. We are now in an age where we have North American Indians with premodern worldviews, modern worldviews, and postmodern worldviews. But amazingly, still, even with all the diversity, there is a significant difference between traditional Native American culture and the predominant Euro-American culture. The differences most striking to me are the differences in worldviews.

Among Native Americans and other Indigenous peoples, there often remains a sense of values that supersede everything else. Even in highly dysfunctional Native American families there exists an unexplained unity about certain ways of being and understandings. I'm not claiming that these ways are always intact. I am not even claiming that these ways of being will survive this century. What I am claiming, after over half a century of my own participatory observation among our Indigenous peoples, is that Native Americans and other Indigenous recipients of modern missions, have something that the dominant American worldview desperately needs, including American missiologists.

Native Americans are known in our society as the "invisible minority" even though when known by others, infamy comes from having the highest alcohol use rates, lowest education levels, highest teen pregnancy rates, highest suicide rates, etc. In a very real sense, because our Indigenous people have been marginalized and disenfranchised for the entire Western history of North America, Native Americans are the quintessential *cultural other* and thus, have something valuable to share. The Western church

Introduction: Apparent Contradictions

needs, and I believe wants (sometimes even without knowing it), what Indigenous people have to offer. As it is, I write from my own experiences, largely among Native Americans, but with much exposure to global citizens and foreign missions and missionaries, as well.

PART 1

Evaluating the Western Missional Paradigm

Chapter One

Confessions of a Missionary Oppressor

"Sometimes it takes a wrong turn to get you to the right place."—Mandy Hale

Have you ever considered the link between evangelism and relationship? At one time I was what you might call a "flaming evangelist." I had trained under every evangelistic program around at the time, including Evangelism Explosion, Billy Graham's KNOCK program of evangelism, Glad Tidings School of Evangelism, and The Four Spiritual Laws. I knocked on doors, witnessed on the streets, set up witnessing booths in shopping malls, set up summer beach evangelism programs, spoke at Jesus festivals, and shared what I believed was the "good news" anywhere I was invited. I took on this lifestyle because that is what I was told it meant to follow Jesus, namely, to tell others about Jesus. Yet, I always wondered why I had within me a constant anxiety that told me I was intruding in someone else's life. According to the evangelical prescription, I "won" hundreds of people "to the Lord." But this did not bring me lasting joy nor did it often seem to "stick" with these converts. Later, many of these people would simply fall away from what I was told it meant to follow Jesus. I knew I lacked something major in my theology and what it meant to follow Jesus; I just didn't know what was missing.

Eventually, I was bothered enough by my conscience to branch out from the strict bubble of evangelicalism, to attend a Christian liberal arts college. There, my view of God was pried open enough to create space for serious self-reflection and critique. I began to think about God differently, which also helped me to see people differently. A more in-depth study of the life of Jesus helped me to understand people and what I think Jesus felt about people, especially those who were most disempowered. Jesus felt compassion and love for the people around him; his message was love, not correct beliefs. Strict orthodoxy belonged to the most rigid sects of the Pharisees in his time, not his followers.

Through deeper questioning and developing knowledge and skills to aid my biblical interpretation, I was able to understand Jesus better, in his own context, and transfer that understanding to broader theological constructs. By understanding Jesus' love for the whole world, demonstrated by his encounters, I came to understand more of who God might be, and that view was very different than the one I held prior. These learnings all helped me understand my own personal encounter with Jesus better.

I think how we view God has a lot to do with how we understand our relationship with our fellow human beings. A God whose primary concern is making sure everyone knows more about him seems entirely egotistical. A God who is most concerned about people's relationship with the world around them, including other people, seems more interesting and more caring and even humble. I found that when I stopped objectifying God, I also stopped objectifying people. I'm sure it worked both ways as well. Really getting to know people helped me to understand God better. People to me were no longer a target, an object of my propaganda, but rather they were like me—frail and fantastic, having both good and bad in them, full of dreams and disappointments. Like me, other people needed healing. I began to understand healing and vulnerability to be endemic to relationship. The more intimate and genuine the relationship, the more opportunities for healing both for them and me: true relationship works both ways.

As I began to rethink what I was told early on as a follower of Jesus, I also wondered how such a lopsided view of humanity, and a distortion of our relationship with God, became normalized. This journey led me into much research and soul-searching. What I discovered in history was equally disturbing to my soul and I had a difficult time coming to grips with my personal journey and mission. After all, I had been a commissioned missionary. I had led hundreds to Christ. I had invested my life and passion into seeing people come to know Jesus.

Way Lost

American Christianity is missing something. Christianity, still by far the predominant religion in America, is declining fast. The church, by and large, has lost its moral influence in society. It is no surprise that a society that now distrusts its most significant institutions of power might also mistrust the church, exactly because it has participated in reflecting a misappropriation of power in many un-Christlike ways. People are angry. They are saying "no" to the hallmarks of American society. Most dissatisfied people just want a government that responds to the voices and concerns of the people. Disenfranchised citizens just want to stop corporate subsidies, graft, and corruption. Most dissatisfied Christians don't want to get rid of meeting together. Disenfranchised followers of Christ just want to stop the hypocrisy and allow power to be used for the good of everyone. The parallel to church and society is that, overall, people want a more just society and more responsive systems.

While many denominations report deep struggles maintaining their preferred state of homeostasis, it may be of interest to know that those people who are departing from their familiar spiritual franchises are not actually leaving the Christian faith. Instead, they are leaving a system that no longer seems to value their spiritual and emotional needs. They want to keep their faith: they just don't want it wrapped in the historic modern American package.

What of those who exit the church? From what I can tell, it appears the "dearly departed" are as alive as ever. I talk to them at colleges and cafes, train stations and internet stations, seminaries and activist organizations, and almost everywhere I can engage in conversations concerning people's spirituality. One characteristic all these people seem to have in common is a sense of loss that is caused by living in the cold, un-nurturing confines of modernity. This is especially so in the modern Western American church. The fact that church is supposed to be a caring entity makes the contrasted coldness of modernity even more obvious. As far as they are concerned, many people feel the modern church is dead, and if not dead, it may take decades, perhaps centuries, for the church to actually transform itself into a meaningful, postcolonial organism, if in fact, that is where the church is headed.

In their attempts to be relevant, the keepers of the state of the modern church resemble the orchestra playing on the deck of the *Titanic* as it slowly sinks into the frozen abyss. Those who have left the church found that padded chairs, pastoral teams, grand stages, Plexiglas pulpits, worship bands, and YouTube clips are doing too little, too late. Not that these things in and of themselves have no purpose, but still, it has become apparent to more and more people that something is missing. Many of the people whom I described long for a true sustaining vision. They are looking for a *sense of place* in which they can become rooted. They are seeking a "tribal" identity in which they find acceptance and authentic identity. They are demanding a voice. They still have their faith, but in a sense, they are lost. They are not lost because they have lost *their* way, but they are lost because *the Way has lost them.*

Today people are lost both in the church and out of the church. They have been awakened enough to have the integrity to admit that they feel less hypocritical when they don't feed into the same broken system that they have come to find irrelevant, ridiculous, and sometimes even despicable. They know the issue is complex, but they also sense the fits of desperation in the modern Western church as it slowly withers in its final death throes.

What happened to American Christianity, with all its gusto and vigor, if it ever existed at all? And, was this passion in some ways misdirected? Perhaps it has something to do with the alienation we discussed earlier. Churches, like other institutions, began to be replaced because people in them have felt helpless. People who needed for their voice to be heard came to realize that they were voiceless. People who wanted to make a difference in their community and even in their world could do neither. So, where did they go?

These "lost people"—or, because they have the courage to be honest, I prefer the term "woke people"—are now searching the arts together at movies and book clubs for a glimpse of God's truth. They are fellowshipping under bridges and serving humanity by giving haircuts and clean socks to the homeless. Some have sought an institution without a history of glaring hypocrisy to the point where they have made using profanity from the pulpit obligatory. Some are just staying at home and getting their news of the outside world from TikTok and Twitter because this affords them easy entry and a point of conversation about the events of the real world. Some have given up on any traditional form of media and rely solely on internet searches and social media feeds for their awareness and their spirituality.

In our overwhelmed expectations, we may neglect to face reality, trying to hold on to something that, in many ways, was a poor model to begin with. Our concerns might be addressed sooner if we simply begin by asking ourselves, "What are the next steps that followers of Jesus will need to make in the twenty-first century, in order to be not just relevant, but prophetic in our world?"

If you have felt a sense of helplessness in what should be considered the most hopeful of all institutions, there is a problem. Even if you felt just a desire to become more active in the world; if you want to feel hopeful and be helpful, would you be willing to try another paradigm, different from the one you have known? If you feel like you can trust me even a smidgen as a worthy guide, to share with you, from what is to you an alternative perspective, just how good God really is, and what God may be saying to your community, then I ask you to join me on a journey that may open up a new way of being and relating to Creator God, to the people around us, and to God's creation, or what I refer to as the whole community of creation. As followers of Jesus, we have the privilege to carry the good news into the world. My prayer is that we simply carry this message in the same spirit in which it was first given by Jesus himself. But first, we must rediscover just what the message we carry is.

Introducing a Few Terms

Shalom: The structured order, or government, of God's love, is not power over others but rather is shalom. What is shalom? Shalom is an ancient Jewish construct of concretizing practical love to be expressed through structures and systems. The structured order or government of God's love is shalom. Shalom is seen in the beauty and balance of the Genesis creation stories. From there, shalom, as seen against the background of the negative, is broken at almost every level in the stories from Genesis 3–11. These examples of broken shalom include the breaks between God and humanity; between marriage partners; between the earth/creation and humanity; between siblings; and in civil society and between neighbors.

Shalom is not simply well-being for ourselves but also creates structured concern that becomes demonstrated on behalf of the poor, disenfranchised, and marginalized, so they may receive empowerment. This concern is expressed often in the Bible for the welfare of widows, orphans, and foreigners. Shalom leaves food out for others during the harvest; it sets aside portions of land to be harvested for those who don't own land. Shalom in Scripture cares for the wild animals and has feasts that include everyone at the same table. Shalom is God's counter-kingdom of inclusion to a power-based empire of exclusion. The shalom kingdom is an available empire of love, not colonizing but offering hope and well-being for any who want to receive and co-create it.

God's love is abundant, including peace, mercy, justice, hospitality, righteousness, restitution, and a whole plethora of characteristics expressed for the individual and for the common good, through both personal and systemic action. Shalom is the ethic Jesus preached and the action he lived as he confronted systems of broken shalom in a shattered and fragmented world. Jesus' constant reference to the "kingdom" (not the actual word he used) was that of a shalom kingdom. The shalom kingdom is not ethereal or utopian in nature, but very real. Shalom can be clearly identified and it is communal in nature, not being satisfied just to seek the good of the individual. Shalom seeks the common good and it benefits the whole community of creation in identifiable and tangible ways.

One very visible path to shalom is when we engage in hospitality, which shalom provides even to one's enemies. Shalom hospitality leads to understanding others. Understanding others leads to acceptance of both our commonalities and differences. Acceptance of these differences leads to caring. Caring leads to community actions that create systems for the well-being of the community, based in equity and equality. These systems and structures provide a guide for shalom living. Similarly, many Indigenous peoples around the world have a shalom construct I refer to generally as the Harmony Way. Systems and structures influence and provide for harmonious (shalom) living.

Harmony Way: A way of living that undergirds all of North American Indigenous history, religion, traditions, ceremonies, stories, philosophy and relationships. Through studying a number of Native American tribes, I argue in my book *Shalom and the Community of Creation: An Indigenous Vision* (2012) that most all of the Native North American tribal peoples shared a common vision and set of values that I call the "Harmony Way." The Harmony Way is found within an Indigenous worldview that encompasses both being and doing in life, according to a set of values that are interconnected and that construct a meaningful whole. Harmonious and reconciled relations with others result when there is a deep ethical respect that characterizes those relationships. The wisdom of Indigenous religious traditions emphasizes the importance of restoring the broken relationships that exist among Creator, humans, each other, animals, and the earth. In many ways, the Harmony Way is akin to, and intersects with, in too many places to name, shalom.

Community of Creation: When I refer to the "community of creation" I have several things in mind. First, is the replacement of that all too familiar imperial side of Christianity sometimes called Christendom. Even though I don't relish the word "kingdom," since I think it is more aligned with what King James wanted rather than what Jesus meant, I always at the least use the term shalom kingdom, because Jesus' understanding of God's kingdom is nothing less than being tied into the whole meta-construct of shalom.[1] Secondly, I want to move into a less anthropocentric idea. Christ incarnates, lives, dies, and resurrects for the whole of creation—not just humanity. I also have a specific hermeneutic of community from which I understand the gospel of Christ, namely, the whole community of creation, which includes everything.

In terms of the use of the word "kingdom," I think Creator cares little about the actual word we use but God does care about how we view the realm of God and how God inhabits the realm we are to spread. To me, community of creation describes this well. At a time when the earth is on the brink of destruction caused by humans, I also feel this description can help us to think of the relationship between our faith and caring for creation, and the global implications mission has in this reality. For instance, right now, the world is having a bee problem. If we lose the bees, we may see worldwide famine beyond what we already experience. Jesus' "kingdom," when thought of as community of creation, speaks directly to this concern in its description.

Indigenous Theology (North American): North American Indigenous theology, done correctly, is in itself a contradiction. The difference between Western, post-Enlightenment theologies and Indigenous North American theologies divides at the level of worldview. Western worldviews tend to concern themselves with tight definitions and extrinsic categorization. Traditional North American Indigenous peoples, and it is from this particular worldview that North American Indigenous theology must be done in order to be bona fide, are cautious to leave room for mystery when speaking of Creator. In fact, in some Native American tribes it is considered taboo to speak too much when trying to define Creator.

North American Indigenous theology speaks *to* Creator more than it does *about* Creator, understanding Creator's sacred presence in everything

---

1. Kingdom is a metaphor that was chosen as an English word to translate the Greek word *basileia*. In his use of *basileia ton theon,* better translated as "a place where God is allowed to be God, having full reign," Jesus pictured shalom. I understand a metaphor as a symbol that translates the meaning of something best into one's context. I, and perhaps many Indigenous peoples (and others) cannot relate to kings and kingdoms except as colonial powers stealing land and bringing destruction. These type of kingdoms forced themselves upon others and perpetuated many of the evil systems of this world. I, along with many others, I suspect, cannot make the transfer symbolically to think of God as a "good king."

and in everyone. In this system of theology, belief is really about doing rather than simply knowing. Given these and other differences in worldviews, perhaps the best North American Indigenous theology can do is to attempt to be a bridge between theological understandings in their cultures without crossing sacred boundaries.

Intercultural Studies: The myth of a singular culture has been important in creating systems suited for empire and to promote racist understandings in all the sciences, including anthropology and missiology. The truth is that we all live in many cultures, even when people's lifeways seem similar. That shared system of lifeways and cultural symbols is what anthropologists have called culture. But even within those shared symbols and lifeways, for instance North American white cultures, anthropologists recognize there are differing cultures of poverty, homelessness, wealth, region, ethnicity, education, and so forth. We attempt to further distinguish them from one another by using terms such as class and station. People coming from these many places share symbols, food, and the like, but they develop not just class differences, but also worldview differences that perceive similar cultures differently. It would be incorrect to say they share a culture, when in fact they share only parts of those cultures. They, like most everyone, are bicultural, multicultural, or intercultural. In this intersectionality we are all parts of many cultures and much damage has been done through the historic holding up of one culture as a measuring rod to assess all others, with presumed objectivity. Intercultural studies takes seriously the differences and intersections of all these cultural aspects.

Missiology: Missiology is the study of mission. Missiology is concerned with every aspect of mission, including who does it, how it is done, where it is done, and its history. Mission is intimately linked to gospel. Unfortunately, modern mission has concentrated on the "sent" aspect of mission to the point of objectifying those to whom we have been sent. Our mission is inviting others into the community of Jesus, whether they recognize him or not, by ever extending the circle of joy and acceptance, and that is the good news we have to share. I often substitute the word *service* for mission in order to ground the term to its most basic meaning. Another word used could be *purpose*. Our purpose is God's purpose in the world.

Now that we have laid out some parameters, have a few terms defined, and you have a better understanding of the person taking you on this journey, let's continue into the realm of missional history in America and find out how a Hawaiian, a couple of Cherokee Indians, and a particular Ivy League school created America's first international missional undertaking.

Questions for Reflecting

1. Discuss the connection between evangelism and relationship: How can they work together, and can they exist separately? If so, describe what that may look like.
2. The church has lost a lot of people experiencing mistrust. Where do you see yourself in relationship with the church at this time?
3. Share your thoughts about shalom. What are some ways shalom can be made real in your community?
4. The phrase "community of creation" includes both humans and non-humans. How do you feel about being categorized with nonhuman species? Do you think Jesus came to earth to restore shalom to the earth and all its creatures, or just human beings? How do you understand the relationship of "the community of creation" to Jesus' use of "kingdom"?

Chapter Two

The Ill-Fated Heathen School Story

Template for Missional Utopianism

> "We can travel back from 'history' to our present lives—known people, familiar places, established routines—but the journey has left its mark."
> —JOHN DEMOS

IN JOHN DEMOS'S BOOK *The Heathen School: A Story of Hope and Betrayal in the Age of the Early Republic*, he gives us a clue, a sort of meta-narrative of what was happening in the minds of those good Christians concerned about mission just shortly after the founding of this country. The essential story began in 1809 when a Hawaiian teenager, Henry Obookiah, ran away and became employed on a ship, eventually finding himself in New England, then supposedly begging the folks at Yale College for an education. Obookiah eventually converted to Christianity and became a sort of symbol or mascot for a foreign mission movement, whose popularity spread like wildfire across New England and beyond.

In a flash of utopianism, a sense that God was doing God's final work by saving the "heathen" in these last days, Henry Obookiah's conversion inspired a vision for many of the key figures whom evangelicals would revere, such as the Dwight brothers, Jeremiah Everts, various Yale students, and others. Much of the Christian community in New England became sympathetic to the idea that "heathen" youth could be civilized through an educational process and Christianized within the American context, then sent back to their own countries as missionaries. The reality of a foreign mission school for the "heathen" at Cornwall, Connecticut developed significantly as Obookiah accompanied preacher-fundraisers on speaking tours throughout New England. Eventually five Hawaiian young men were enrolled and, not surprisingly, donations to the presiding denomination, the American Board of Commissioners for Foreign Mission, more than doubled.

Subsequently, building and living quarters were erected and young "heathen" students were sought and enrolled, including students from Hawaii, China, India, and Native America. Not all the students took to the role of being Christianized in the way of Henry Obookiah. In fact, of the initial fifty students enrolled, only sixteen completed the full course of study. Students dropped out for reasons of homesickness, difficulty in learning English, drunkenness, and just plain old resentment for the way they were treated by their white handlers. Still, the "Heathen School" at Cornwall understood itself as a success.

These foreign students were under strict supervision, not allowed to go to town or receive guests. They went to school most of the day and were required to work for the school or for the farm two and one-half days per week. Each was assigned their group of "protectors" or handlers, and there is some indication that all the nitpicking paternalism did not sit well with the students. Tamoree, a Hawaiian student who left the school, wrote to his handler saying, "You did not let me attend the schools I had ought . . . You used me like a dog more than a human being . . . You are a base, dirty, mean, low, shameful, poor, avaricious rascal . . . If you ever come within my reach, I would level you to the face of the earth."[1] Clearly, some of the students did not easily accept their objectification.

The temperature of New Englanders began to run hotter when a young Cherokee Indian student named John Ridge fell in love with Sarah Northrup, a daughter of a prominent New England family. Under much scrutiny and disappointment to the community, the two married in 1824. Two years later, Ridge's cousin, Elias Boudinot, repeated the pattern, marrying Harriet Gould. Even though the two Cherokee students were from very elite Cherokee families, it was the last straw for the local white community. Both of these marriages scandalized the white families of Cornwall and even changed the hearts of the school's closest allies. The community's reactions were severe, blaming the Northrups for opening up such a scandalous enterprise for others to follow, calling for Northrup to be "publicly

---

1. Quoted in Demos, *Heathen School*, 41–42.

whipped, the Indians hung, and the mothers drown'd."[2] The Mission School's governing board dubbed Gould and Boudinot's union "criminal," and the whole town gathered under the call of the church bells to hang and burn the couple in effigy. The figures were torched by Harriet Gould's brother.

The school, completely scandalized, officially closed its doors in 1826. The message was clear: we can accept you foreigners as objects of our mission, as mascots, as poster children, as examples of our great accomplishments, but you can never be fully human like us, and you certainly cannot date or marry our daughters! This American hubris among those mission-minded folks was nothing less than full-throated white supremacy under the cover of Christian mission. Unfortunately, not much has changed. The language is now softer. Missionary methods usually have more tact these days, but the hubris is the same. The cultural other is still the "project" of modern mission, worthy of conversion but never quite as human as the missionary (or the missionary's daughters!).

What if? As a student of history, I tend to think in terms of "what if?" What if white people had come to this country with an open view of learning from Native Americans? What if the Westerners had viewed Indigenous people as equals? What if the foreign missionary project to *the cultural other* was based on respect, equality, and equity instead of genocide, land theft, and creating a sub-level category of human beings? We may never know the full answers to these questions, but knowing both cultures well, I can easily surmise that the outcomes for America's Indigenous people would have been much brighter. In fact, in terms of respect for Christianity, it could not be much dimmer.

For over five hundred years Native Americans and other Indigenous peoples around the world have been told by both government and church that their cultures are inferior to those of the Europeans, and that they must abandon their own Indigenous cultures in order to be accepted by society and by God. As my late friend Richard Twiss used to say concerning white missionaries' attitudes and practices to *the cultural other*, "God loves you, but God doesn't really like you!" Even today, with proof that this message is outdated and ineffective in presenting Jesus among Indigenous peoples, many—indeed most indigenous religious learning institutions and churches—still subscribe to some form of this patently inhumane and paternalistic philosophy.

---

2. Quoted in Demos, *Heathen School*, 154.

The Ill-Fated Heathen School Story

The result of past paternalism has been a type of cultural ethnocide in America, which has produced only a small percentage of Native Americans who claim to follow Jesus. Some studies have estimated as low as 3 percent of all Native Americans nationwide are Christians. Those Native churches that do exists are, by and large, often expressing a poor imitation of a bad European model, consisting of all the symptoms of a dying church. Why? Past mission efforts have not spoken to the hearts of Native Americans. Native American values and learning styles speak to the heart. European churches speak to the mind, prioritizing correct doctrine and orderly subjugation, expressing little freedom of thought and life. Fortunately, there are now numerous Native Americans who have found it more important to follow Jesus than European Christianity. And there are those brave traditionalists who have held out for these many years, who understand Jesus as he has been revealed in their own cultures.

My wife and I have done a lot of traveling over years. Four of those years we traveled from reservation to reserve across the United States and Canada, and we mentored a number of Native leaders. We also did a lot of speaking during those four years. We homeschooled our three kids, and as a family we had the incredible experience of our family hanging around with Native people from almost every region of Turtle Island. Among these times were some of the richest experiences of our lives. I told the following story to a group of academics in Wolfville, Nova Scotia, at the famous Hayward Lectures. I would like to repeat it here.

The Story: How I Learned That Jesus Is a Great Spirit

We've been doing Native American work, serving our own Indigenous peoples, for over thirty years. I consider those years the most valuable times among all my learning experiences. I'm going to share a story with you from those years because I know Canada has a wonderful practice of recognizing the host peoples of the land. Wherever we went to speak, we always sought the blessing of the host people on whose land we were on because that's what we were taught by our elders. So, we were going to the Ojibwa reservation near Hayward, Wisconsin. When I got there, I asked the group that had invited me, the YWAM (Youth with a Mission) Native leadership base, "Who welcomed you on the land?"

They had invited us to come up for a week and teach an Indigenous leadership course, so I wanted to be sure all was being done in a good way.

Unfortunately, no one had really invited them on the land, so I said, "Well then, we can't speak." This type of problem has actually occurred a couple of different times, but we've always been able to work through it. Creator has always made a way for us to receive the local blessing and speak. But in Hayward, we had just learned of the problem, so we had to tell our host that we won't speak unless the host people welcomed us somehow.

Now, it just so happened that day that this young Ojibwa kid from Seattle, not yet in his twenties, was hitchhiking on the reservation. The young man and his brother were adopted out when he was about two years old and were raised in Seattle by a white family. He had recently experienced an LSD trip during which he saw Jesus, and Jesus told him, "I want you to go back to your reservation." The young man knew he was from a reservation somewhere, way out in Wisconsin. Well, coincidentally the director of the YWAM base saw him hitchhiking on the road and picked him up. The director asked him if he knew who his people were, but he did not. He told Dave, the director of the YWAM base, that while on LSD, Jesus told him to come out here. Then Dave asked if he had any place to stay. He did not. Dave told him he could stay with them, so they fed him and gave him shelter. We got there later that same day.

Naturally, I took the opportunity to include this Ojibwe young man and had him stick with me all day so he could learn something from it. I knew enough to know that he wasn't there by accident. "I want to teach you some things," I told him, and he said, "Okay." I told him whenever we go to someone else's land, even now, my elders told me, even when driving down the road, to stop and put tobacco down, because that is someone else's land and we need to respect it. But to be completely honest, I need to tell you that when driving I haven't always done that, just because we travel through so many places, we'd be stopping constantly. But we have asked for permission wherever we teach or exercise any sort of spiritual influence. And so, it was important that we did it right that day, especially now that we had a young person trying to find himself and his Indigenous identity. After some thought was given to this, we figured out who the elder we should speak with was. He was one of the two leaders of the Midewiwin lodge, their tribal religion, and he was also a tribal elder and elder representative to the tribal council.

We went to the local store and we made a traditional elder basket that consisted of flour and tobacco, a flashlight and coat hangers, sugar and coffee, fresh fruit, and all the kinds of things that elders like. After tracking down his address, we went to the elder's house and knocked on the door, and his wife answered. I guess people visit him often for advice, so she very naturally said, "Oh, come on and set the basket down, he's on the phone right now." Finally, he came back and asked respectfully, "Who are you guys and what do you want?" I explained to him who we were and that we were going to be teaching on spiritual matters to Indigenous leaders there. He said, "Well, what are you going to be teaching?" I explained how we do things according to our traditional teachings, but we follow Jesus. We were calling it "contextual Native ministry" at the time, but I don't really think of it like that anymore. We just live the life we are supposed to be living. Now we're just Indians being Indians.

Then he started telling us some pretty interesting stories. He said, "You know what you all believe and what we believe is not that different?" Then he told us of a couple of subtle differences concerning hell and the devil. He said, "You know, when I was a younger person, I wanted to find out what you Christians believe, so I enrolled for a semester in this college. It's called Moody Bible Institute, you ever heard of that?" We were surprised and talked about that for some time. But every now and then he would keep interrupting his own story, which meant he was trying to get a point across, and he said, "You know, my uncle told me to never disrespect Jesus, because Jesus is a great spirit and I talk to him." And he would go on and he'd tell us more and more, and then he would say this thing about his uncle again. He told us about how he had just come back from a big meeting of Gichi Dowan, big medicine people from around the United States and Canada. These Ojibwa spiritual leaders were all trying to decide how they could get along better with the Christians. And he told us some stories about all this.

We sat there for maybe two hours, and at least six or seven times he said this thing about his uncle and respecting Jesus. Then, at one point he said, "My uncle trained most of the spiritual leaders around this area. He lived to be over a hundred years old, and my uncle would tell me all these stories about Jesus. So, I asked my uncle one time, I said, 'Uncle, how do you know all this about Jesus? Did you go to residential school?' He said, 'Oh no! No! I never did that.' Then I asked him, 'Did the priest teach you?' And he says, 'No, I have never been to church.' Then I said, 'But you tell me all the stuff about Jesus. Have you been reading the Bible?' My uncle said, 'No, just remember what I told you in the past: don't disrespect Jesus 'cause he's a great spirit, and I talk to him.' I said to my uncle, 'Well, yeah, you talk to him, but how do you know all these things he's done?' You know my uncle looked at me so quizzically, and then he said, 'Well, when I talk to him, of course he talks back.'" And finally the elder said, 'I'm going to pray for you now,' and then our time was over."[3]

I share that original oral story with you because in the European Christian tradition, God and Jesus and the work of the Spirit have been limited to what councils and magisteriums have determined. Beyond that, everyone is expected to color within the lines. My experience has shown me that the lines are restrictive, confining, determinative, and even false. God is much greater than what Western Christianity has ever discovered.

Turtle Island (Listen to the Elders)

I love to travel in North America, or what Indigenous people call Turtle Island, because it offers unparalleled travel adventures of history and geography, social settings and intersecting cultures. Wherever one travels in Turtle Island you are sure to find places where North American Indigenous people made their homes or their living, or both. Why is it called Turtle Island? Several tribes have a story that explains the importance of this phrase. I will share the Chickamauga Cherokee version I learned. Although I have heard this story told by others, I have a particular fondness for the way Cherokee storyteller Robert Francis relays the story (used with permission).

> When the earth was first made, it was covered all over with water except for one small island. This island was the top of a high mountain. This was Blue Mountain, in the Cherokee country. White folks came a short time ago and named this mountain Clingman's Dome, no doubt after some white man or other named Clingman. But it has always been Blue Mountain and always will be Blue Mountain. For the Cherokees, the Ani-Kituwa, the Ani-Yunwiya, this is where it begins.
>
> Everyone lived together on this mountaintop island. The human beings and the animals all got along fine. In those days they could understand one another's speech, for this was before the humans broke the harmony. The animals were also much bigger in those days. In fact, the animals of today are but shadows of those who once were. It was a good place to live. Sure, the island was small, but it was what everyone knew and was used to. All were

---

3. Transcribed from the 2019 Hayward Lectures, Woodley, "Indigenous Worldview as Original Instructions and a Critique of the Western Worldview."

The Ill-Fated Heathen School Story

content, until there came to be more of them than the small bit of land could support.

As they noticed they were getting crowded, a general council of all the people (both humans and animals) was called. The question was asked, "What can we do?" The only answer given was, "We can pray. All we can do is pray and ask the Grandfather Above to please give us some more land."

So, all the people prayed, and Creator/Apportioner answered, "Oh my precious children, there is nothing I enjoy so much as giving good gifts to my children. But if I do everything for you without asking you to help in any way, how will you ever learn any responsibility? I really want to teach you some responsibility. Here's what I will do: If one of you will swim to the bottom of the ocean and bring up some mud, just a little bit of mud, I will take that mud, that little bit of mud, and make a whole great land of it."

All the people (animals and humans) began to look at one another. Someone asked, "Who will go? Who will get the mud?"

A slow, deep voice answered, "I will go. I will get the mud." It was Grandma Turtle.

"Grandma Turtle, you can't go!" They said, "You're too old and slow. We don't know what it's like down there. We don't know how deep it is."

"I'll go," quacked Duck.

"Now that's more like it," they said. "You're a good swimmer, Duck. You can go; you can do it."

Duck paddled out onto the ocean and dived, but he popped right back up to the surface. Duck dived again and again and again, but the same thing happened each time. Well, you know how ducks are. They dive well, but they float much better. Duck paddled back to shore, shook the water off his tail and said, "I can't dive that deep. I float too well."

The question was asked again, "Who will go? Who will get the mud?"

Grandma Turtle said, "I will go. I will get the mud."

"Grandma Turtle," they said, "we settled that before! You can't go. You're too old. Who will go? Who will get the mud? Hey Otter, how about you?"

"What?" Otter said.

"How about you going to get the mud?"

"Mud? What mud?"

"The mud we need so Creator/Apportioner can make more land!"

"Oh, sure," said Otter, and he slid off into the water and was gone a good long while. When he came back, he had a fish in his mouth, but no mud. Without a word to anyone, Otter climbed up onto the beach and began munching on the fish.

Everyone was watching him, but Otter paid them no mind, just kept eating his fish. "Hey Otter!" someone yelled.

"What?" Otter said.

"Where's the mud?"

"Mud? What mud?" Otter asked. "Ohhh, the mud! Well, I left here to go and get it. Then I got started playing. Then I caught this fish. Then I forgot all about the ummm, ummmm, whatever it was I was supposed to get."

Oh my! They were nearly at their wits' end. "Who will go?" they all asked. "Who will get the mud?"

Grandma Turtle said, "I will go. I will get the mud." No one even paid her any mind.

"Who will go? Who will get the mud?"

"I will go," said Beaver. "I will get the mud. I don't play, and I do not eat fish."

Resolutely, Beaver swam out into the ocean. He took a deep, deep breath and dived. Wow, Beaver was gone a long time. Some of the people watching and waiting were holding their breath in sympathy, but none seemed able to hold it that long. Finally, Beaver popped to the surface gasping for air. He swam to shore and climbed onto the beach shaking his head. "It's too deep!" Beaver said. "I don't know how deep it is. I never reached the bottom."

Everyone was in despair. Beaver was the last best hope. How would they ever get mud? Maybe there would never be anything but the little mountaintop island. "Who will go?" they asked. "Who will get the mud?"

A slow, deep voice answered, "I will go. I will get the mud."

"You can't go, Grandma Turtle, you're too . . ."

"I WILL GO! I WILL GET THE MUD!"

There were no other volunteers, so they let Grandma Turtle go. She slowly paddled her way out onto the surface of the ocean. As everyone watched, she took a slow, deep breath, then another and another and another. She took three more breaths and disappeared beneath the water.

They waited a long time. Grandma Turtle was gone much longer than Duck or Otter or even Beaver had been. She was gone all that day and the next and the next and the next. They posted a sentry up on the very top of the mountain. Finally, on the seventh day, the sentry called out, "I think I see something coming up. Yes,

yes, something is rising in the water. Could it be? Could it be? Yes! It's Grandma Turtle!"

Sure enough, Grandma Turtle rose to the surface of the ocean, and there she lay, not moving, with her legs, her tail, her head all hanging down.... Grandma Turtle was dead.

Quietly, reverently, Duck, Otter, and Beaver swam out and drew Grandma Turtle's body to the shore. They pulled her up on the beach, as all the people (humans and animals) gathered sadly around, and what's this? There, under her front feet, they found ... mud.

Someone pried the mud from Grandma Turtle's claws and rolled it into a ball and lifted it up toward the sky. The Grandfather took that mud, that little bit of mud, and cast it out, making this whole, great land that many nations call Turtle Island, making it into the shape of a Turtle in honor of Grandma Turtle's sacrifice.

Indigenous people, even Indian children, are not surprised to hear that in this story, Grandmother Turtle's actions turn out to be those that save the community. She represents the oldest and wisest of the group. They understand that the situation will not improve until the elder is heard and her suggestions are heeded. Authority from Indigenous elders comes through reflected experience. The idea here is that we can trust our elders and our traditions to lead us onto a good path. The Cherokee story of the expansion of the world has many teaching points, but primary among them is that we should listen first to those among us who are the oldest, because their wisdom is based upon much reflected experience. And in Indian country, truth is not simply knowledge, but knowledge exercised and lived. Our Indigenous elders have been on this land since time immemorial, passing down wisdom and knowledge and stories and ceremonies and songs that make the connections between human beings and Creator and the whole community of creation. It's time to listen. It's time the "what if" becomes the question, "what now?"

Questions for Reflecting:

1. In what ways was "the Heathen School" a template for early American missions? In what ways can utopianism be harmful? Do you think Christianity is a utopian-based religion? Explain your response.

2. Richard Twiss used to say concerning the attitudes and practices of white missionaries to the cultural other, "God loves you, but God doesn't really like you!" Make a list and share it, of all the ways this could happen in a cross-cultural missional situation.

3. Share some of the implications you deduced from the story of the elder and Jesus as a great Spirit. How might this affect your own theology?

4. In the story of Grandmother Turtle, where did you imagine yourself to fit in? What are additional conclusions that might be drawn from the story?

Chapter Three

Beyond Western Missional Hegemony

The History We Carry

"Savages we call them, because their manners differ from ours, which we think the perfection of civility; they think the same of theirs."
—Benjamin Franklin

The Foundations of Missio Americana

THERE WAS AN ERA, well actually more than one era, when brave, young, white men would stand up among their peers to answer the call of "mission to the heathen." In each American generation that stance has looked a bit different, but the root is the same. The call was most often couched in terms that showed concern for the seemingly poor, unsaved, uneducated, and uncivilized people who had not yet reaped the benefits of proper Western civilization or Christianization. Thus, in 1898 none would express it so succinctly as the Victorian era poet and storyteller, encouraging US imperialism in the Philippines by writing to his friend Theodore Roosevelt, who had just been elected governor of New York.

Joseph Rudyard Kipling, who penned *The Jungle Book*, "Rikki-Tikki-Tavi," and "The Man Who Would Be King," would never live to fathom how much disgust and ire he would garner from later generations for such a poem as "The White Man's Burden." Kipling's well-intended thoughts give us keen insight into the mindset present in America's colonial past, which is inseparable from her missional past. Unfortunately, for those on the receiving end of colonial missions, the confident consciousness of white supremacy that has fueled America's missional past remains ubiquitous and central to today's missional efforts.

> Take up the White Man's burden—
> Send forth the best ye breed—
> Go send your sons to exile
> To serve your captives' need
> To wait in heavy harness
> On fluttered folk and wild—
> Your new-caught, sullen peoples,
> Half devil and half child
> Take up the White Man's burden
> In patience to abide
> To veil the threat of terror
> And check the show of pride;
> By open speech and simple
> And hundred times made plain
> To seek another's profit
> And work another's gain
> Take up the White Man's burden—
> And reap his old reward:
> The blame of those ye better
> The hate of those ye guard—
> The cry of hosts ye humour
> (Ah slowly) to the light:
> "Why brought ye us from bondage,
> Our loved Egyptian night?"
> Take up the White Man's burden—
> Have done with childish days—
> The lightly proffered laurel,
> The easy, ungrudged praise.
> Comes now, to search your manhood
> Through all the thankless years,
> Cold-edged with dear-bought wisdom,
> The judgment of your peers![1]

In Kipling's pen lay the core of the matter: the presumed burden of the white man to lift up those of presumed lower stature, to the heights of Western European and Euro-American standards. In that notion lies the truth of mission to the "benighted savages," the "foreign-born wretch," and the "poor and destitute" in America. Perhaps it may be considered cruel to

1. Kipling, "White Man's Burden."

blame Kipling's poetry as something other than a noble attempt to raise the standards. He, after all, was simply a person of his time. Perhaps the immensely talented Kipling should not be faulted for what he assumed were his noble thoughts. These same thoughts, the same attitude, were on the minds of many a well-intentioned white man, regardless of the era, but they still remain today. Kipling's concerns of the white man's burden are embedded in the plight of this nation, and other nations around the world.

America's Founding White Fathers

Mission, some would correctly argue, was intentionally included in the preliminary purpose and documents, even before the founding of what would be called the "New World." The Virginia, Connecticut, and Massachusetts charters were each drawn up showing concern for the Indigene whom, by the way, they had never seen. In other words, the mission of the "gospel" was already in their minds before they ever set foot on the shores of the new continent. But what was their concern?

> First Charter of Virginia, April 10, 1606
>
> We, greatly commending, and graciously accepting of, their [the colonists'] Desires for the Furtherance of so noble a Work, which may, by the Providence of Almighty God, hereafter tend to the Glory of his Divine Majesty, in propagating of Christian Religion to such People, as yet live in Darkness and miserable Ignorance of the true Knowledge and Worship of God, and may in time bring the Infidels and Savages, living in those parts, to human Civility, and to a settled and quiet Government: DO, by these our Letters Patents, graciously accept of, and agree to, their humble and well-intended Desires.[2]
>
> The Charter of the Massachusetts Bay Colony, 1629
>
> . . . whereby our said People, Inhabitants there, may be soe religiously, peaceablie, and civilly governed, as their good Life and orderlie Conversacon, maie wynn and incite the Natives of Country, to the Knowledg and Obedience of the onlie true God and Saulor of Mankinde, and the Christian Fayth.[3]

---

2. https://avalon.law.yale.edu/17th_century/va01.asp#1.
3. https://avalon.law.yale.edu/17th_century/mass03.asp.

Charter of Connecticut, 1662

> ... whereby Our said People Inhabitants there, may be so religiously, peaceably and civilly governed, as their good Life and orderly Conversation may win and invite the Natives of the Country to the Knowledge and Obedience of the only true GOD, and He Saviour of Mankind, and the Christian Faith, which in Our Royal Intentions, and the adventurers free Possession, is the only and principal End of this Plantation ... and to take or surprize by all Ways and Means whatsoever, all and every such Person and Persons, with their Ships' Armour, Ammunition and other Goods of such as shall in such hostile Manner invade or attempt the defeating of the said Plantation, or the hurt of the said Company and Inhabitants, and upon just Causes to invade and destroy the Natives, or other Enemies of the said Colony.[4]

The name-calling, so apparent to us today, such as "Infidels," "Savages," those living "in darkness," those "ignorant of the truth," all reveal the common prejudicial thinking inherent to Europeans at the time, and unveil the heinous link between civilization and Christianization. To the European, and later to Euro-Americans, there was no space between the two constructs. The link I mention continues to be an unspoken rule in American mission, even today. Missionaries in that era believed that teaching primitive people about a "better" way of living was part of the gospel message. Evangelization and civilization could not be separated. You could tell if an Indian was being saved from hell by the way he or she began to live like the English.[5]

Mission among America's Aborigines served as a template in regard to missionary attitudes across the world. The same white supremacy reflected by those early settlers on America's shores, especially apparent among missionaries to Native Americans, was exhibited in Africa, India, and beyond. Regardless of the century, missionaries echoed the attitude of the US government. The missionaries may have been after the "souls" of the native but make no mistake, their mission was fully integrated with the government's goal of assimilation.

Long considered America's "apostle to the Indians," John Elliot worked in tandem with the Puritan cause to commit "cultural genocide in all its social, economic, political and religious aspects."[6] Elliot's views reflected

---

4. https://avalon.law.yale.edu/17th_century/ct03.asp.
5. Beaver, *Introduction to Native American Church History*, 49.
6. Tinker, *Missionary Conquest*, 21.

those of his day: "As for these poore Indians, they have no principles of their own, not yet wisdom of their own. (I mean as other Nations have.)"[7] Elliot's understanding at the time reflected the pervasive view that without Western European-based civilization, there could be no Christian manifestation. Elliot's idea of the Praying Towns for Indians, which attempted to impart all the strict puritanical rigor accompanying the Puritan ethic, while at the same time keeping Indians segregated, provided the Puritans the dual purpose of pride in their exhibition of Indians, who were an example of colonial assimilation, and a physical buffer between the Puritan colonies and the threat of attack from hostile Native American forces. In other words, the cost of assimilation to the Christianized Indigenous people of New England was not only the loss of their culture and lifeways, but often the cost of their very lives.

In the eighteenth century Jonas Michaelius, an early Dutch missionary in Manhattan, New York, echoed the common sentiment.

> As to the Natives of this country, I find them entirely savage and wild, strangers to all decency, yea, uncivil and stupid as garden poles, proficient in all wickedness and godlessness; devilish men, who serve nobody but the Devil.[8]

Michaelius's sentiment was shared by missionaries to Native Americans throughout the era. The simple phrase "stupid as garden poles," or sometimes "dumb as garden poles," was a common descriptor used by missionaries in eighteenth-century literature while describing Indigenous people. The same language was used overseas as well. It expresses the presumed white superiority of the day.

In the nineteenth century, famed missionary Isaac McCoy penned a book endorsing Indian removal and supporting a form of colonization. McCoy, in some ways, is a progenitor of the current Indian reservation system. McCoy's idea of an "Indian Canaan" served the purposes of Western expansion, Indian removal, and was endorsed by Andrew Jackson.[9] At the time, many Anglo-Americans thought Indians incapable of improvement or civilization, according to the white man's standards. Andrew Jackson's secretary of state, Henry Clay, wrote a treatise against Indians, published in 1827, epitomizing a common view:

---

7. Tinker, *Missionary Conquest*, 21.
8. Quoted in Gaustad, *Documentary History of Religion in America*, 83.
9. McLoughlin, *Champions of the Cherokees*, 119.

> It is impossible to civilize Indians. There was never a full-blooded Indian that ever took to civilization. It is not in their nature. They are a race destined for extinction . . . I do not think they are, as a race, worth preserving.[10]

Andrew Jackson and Henry Clay's intention was, as was for most of those in power of the day, to use proper force to ensure the Indians' removal. The reservation system, still in its nascent stages, like the ill-fated Praying Towns, was used to remove Native people from white civilization, serving a multitude of purposes, including providing opportunities for the theft of their land, removing them so they don't become a reminder of centuries of the white man's failure in their attempts to civilize and Christianize them, and to relegate them to the hinterlands where they would slowly fade from existence without intervention. The rationale was always "it's for their own good." Whether the intentions were altruistic or evil (I think evil with altruism used as a rationale), the thrust of Western civilization was to make Indians disappear. The purpose of making America's Indigene obsolete was manifold: to make land available to whites, to absolve themselves of the guilt for the treacherous ways that the land was stolen, to rationalize cultural cannibalism, and to mythologize the "noble savage." Ultimately, the goal, which is the invariable goal of white supremacy in the history of America, was to create white space and protect that space at all costs.

Twentieth-century mission to the American Indian continued with the same rationale but adopted more temperate language when describing Indians. The sentiments were, nonetheless, the same, expressing a deep-seated formulation of white supremacy, whether through the doctrine of discovery, manifest destiny, residential Indian boarding schools, lack of funding for Indian health, housing, and education, or bureaucratic laws of governance. These same Euro-American, white supremacists values have served to educate Christian denominations well into the present era.

G. E. E. Lindquist, in a 1951 missionary handbook, demonstrates this common lack of concern and naiveté among the many denominations and mission agencies concerning any possibility of doing mission using Native American values. Lindquist's message discouraged missionaries from using even the most basic cultural value of language as a common bond: "Do not spend too much time trying to learn the language . . . If the Indians among whom you are to work do not speak English, they will soon do so."[11]

---

10. McLoughlin, *Champions of the Cherokees*, frontispiece.

11. Lindquist, *New Trails*, 33.

Ultimately, the goal of Christian mission was civilization. Misconceptions about Indigenous cultures and the forced imposition of conforming to white civilization still reflect the government's goals of assimilation. The missionary, either knowingly or unknowingly, has most often played into the government's hand as a full partner. Nowhere in American history is this malignant partnership more apparent than in the tragic story of the residential Indian boarding schools.

The Residential Indian Boarding Schools

Native American residential boarding schools were a planned attempt to educate and civilize American Indians in the late nineteenth century, lasting up until the late twentieth century. I had never heard the personal stories of boarding school survivors until I was sent as a missionary to Anadarko, Oklahoma by my denomination. I had been educated in a general sense about the horrors of the residential Indian boarding schools years earlier, but to hear what actually happened as told by those elders who survived was another thing altogether.

Anadarko is sometimes called the "Indian Capital of the Nation." There are seventeen tribes located within a forty-mile radius of Anadarko and there is always some kind of event or ceremony happening within that hub. Although I had been a missionary among Native Alaskans prior, I began my missionary experience in Anadarko by making a formal request from my denomination. I asked for a letter to accompany me, apologizing to the tribes for my denomination's participation in the boarding schools, along with a complete repudiation of white supremacy. To make a long story short, the letter was never granted.

Native American residential boarding schools were an effort between the United States government and Christian denominations to "civilize the Indian." The enterprise was nothing short of ethnocide and some have even referred to it as attempted genocide.[12] Having spent long hours listening to the stories of elders who were boarding school survivors around Anadarko and, later, all over the United States and Canada, I find their stories remarkably similar. Many speak of being forced to attend school a few hours a day, forced into daily labor while wearing itchy wool uniforms, and in military fashion, lining up in silence to bells and whistles all day long.

---

12. See Churchill, *Little Matter of Genocide*.

Mission and the Cultural Other

In the United States the government sponsored the schools with direct employment and assistance from the denominations. In Canada it was the opposite. The Canadian government assisted the Christian denominations. Most often it was the missionary or the Indian agent who either suggested or coerced Native American families to send their children to the boarding schools. These efforts were done in a number of ways, including the promises of education, good standing with God and the church, or even food, supplies, and perhaps an income. Conversely, threats were often made concerning eternal damnation, cutting off rations, and even forced kidnapping to make the children attend the schools. Thus, the thread of Christianity and government working together purposefully continued in the formation of this country as it had from the start.

Although there are some elders who will say none of the following things happened to them personally, the number of elders with whom I have heard horror stories from personally is astounding. Invariably, children were malnourished and even starved, sometimes resulting in dysentery and, eventually, death. The number of graves in boarding school cemeteries is remarkable and as discovered recently in Canada, many more children were buried unofficially and hidden from sight.[13] Children in these schools were not allowed to speak their own language and were punished severely when caught doing so. Punishment included strappings, extreme isolation, public humiliation, mouths washed out with lye soap, and beatings. The regimen of punishments at these schools was nothing less than torture. What was worse were the unofficial depredations.

The children who were forced to attend these schools were aged from five to seventeen, with some exceptions. They were separated into male and female dorms with little to no contact with the students of the other gender. I am not overstating the facts to say that sexual abuse from clergy, matrons and patrons, and later, from older students who had been abused themselves, was commonplace. Simply stated, little boys and girls were both raped and made to perform oral sex at alarming rates. Oftentimes this form of sexual slavery continued for years. The results, whether during their captivity or much later in life, were shame, guilt, and self-depredation leading to abusive behaviors such as alcoholism and often suicide. The residential boarding schools, approved and endorsed by the government and Christian denominations alike, exhibited white supremacy in its fullest form, the effects of which continue to devastate Native American communities all

---

13. Newton, "'Unthinkable' discovery."

over the United States and Canada. Similar expressions and sentiments are found wherever in the world North American mission has been established.

Civil Religion

I was privileged to be alive and a participant/observer of history as I watched the anti-apartheid movement grow in the US and around the world, until it finally created significant change. The struggle was real and costly to those who lived through it. The late missiologist David Bosch observed the struggle from the inside while we watched and waited from our somewhat safe shore in America. To be clear-eyed in such turbulent times is a weighty task. Most white Americans could look across the waters to see the injustice being perpetuated in South Africa through the apartheid system. But when it came to our own unique systems of racial oppression, their view was clouded and the task seemed much more difficult. Whether apartheid South Africa or the unique forms of American racial oppression, like Jim Crow or manifest destiny, they share commonality; namely, they sanctify their racism with the blessing of both church and state, with the goal being white supremacy.

> Manifest destiny is a product of nationalism.... The result of this was that, at one point or another in recent history, virtually every white nation regarded itself as being chosen for a particular destiny and as having a unique charisma.... Following as it did, in the wake of the Revivals, it was only natural that it acquired very clear religious overtones and also that it would soon be wedded to the foreign mission enterprise.[14]

Civil religion is perhaps the most pervasive, deepest held, and ubiquitous religious belief in the United States. It runs deep and is held dear to many white Americans, but the marriage of religious fervor and nationalism dates back to the most ancient of societies. The US is not the first nation to wrap Jesus in their flag, but we certainly have developed our own unique culture around the process. The unique expression of what John L. O'Sullivan coined as a phrase in 1845, as America's "manifest destiny," was simply more of the same white supremacy found in its predecessor, the doctrine of discovery. Western expansion, an enterprise fully embraced by missionary and government alike, was simply more land stolen from

---

14. Bosch, *Transforming Mission*, 298–300.

Native Americans, more justification for the expansion of West African chattel slavery, and a seeming reinforcement of rationale for the oppression of the cultural other.

> Looking back upon the entire phenomenon of "manifest destiny" and mission, in North American and elsewhere, one has to beware of facile deductions. Both those who insist (as some mission apologists still do) that the missionary flame's ignition was purely religious, and those who, for whichever reasons, contend that it was merely a matter of national identity or expansiveness, miss the point that, only too often, the religious and the national impulses were fundamentally not separable.[15]

The Lingering Spirit of Manifest Destiny

Americans learn by what they were taught from teachers and from years of studying myriad books. Knowledge, to white Western Europeans and Americans, comes most often by simply reading what others have written. Today, Western epistemology is supplemented by what we view through television, movies, documentaries, and social media. Yet, even Western epistemologies are shifting today, and we are not quite sure where that change is taking us.

Gen Xers, millennials, and Gen Zers are asking for a new paradigm other than the one handed down to them by their parents and grandparents. They are examining the old ethnocentric epistemologies and hoping to create a new paradigm that will form their spiritualities and, for those who remain in the church, their missional concerns. Unfortunately, like the old adage goes, the previous generations are "cutting off their nose to spite their face" and those new ways of thinking are being met with resistance. These younger generations are not only looking for a new America that is not laden with racial and ethnic epitaphs and stereotypes, they are looking for a new Jesus who is free from manifest destiny and American exceptionalism.

America's current divisions have deep roots in the philosophical theories of Enlightenment-bound men such as Descartes, Bacon, Grotius, Rousseau, Hobbs, Locke, and Adam Smith. While we now consider their views of distinguishing between what are savage and advanced societies to be racist, they theorized and categorized their opinions with markers of

---

15. Bosch, *Transforming Mission*, 302.

advanced societies being those displaying dualisms, extreme individualism, and intense notions concerning property ownership. In other words, they felt their own European civilization was entering into the highest form of progress and displaying the best forms of human nature. Native Americans, Africans, East Indians, and others, according to these men, were among the lower forms of societies. This cultural "otherizing" was used to justify the classifications into social and "scientific" oppression of other peoples who were not Western European.

Of course, these European philosophers drew water from the wells of Greek philosophers, and they all had tremendous influence on the American founders such as Washington, Jefferson, and Adams, whose ideas and policies reflected the same familiar stereotypes and images that Western civilization had been spouting for several millennia. The idea of the United States arose from such false notions of what is a good society, and today, we can clearly see it as racist. But seeing is often not enough. These cultural distinctions are now "baked into the bread" of American thinking, including how Americans imagine mission and the cultural other.

Perhaps defending the missionaries will be the final vestige of American exceptionalism. After all, some missionaries suffered greatly in their sacrifice, risking life and limb for the furtherance of the gospel. Yet others helped to create the missionary industrial complex by plastering photos of Black or brown babies in their newsletters, with denominations and mission-sending agencies reposting them in their magazines and promotional materials because of their fundraising appeal. Realistically, it was often both. Most missionaries, from my own observations, would find themselves wading in both sides of that pool.

The great missional cover-up remains yet to be fully exposed. As I have shared my own experiences among Native Americans with other missionaries from around the world, they have confirmed similar experiences to mine and worse. And this in spite of the fact that I must have heard a hundred times the retort from churchgoers, "at least we did mission well in foreign countries." The lie undergirding colonial missional attitudes and practices that were wrought by Americans and other Western peoples, must be exposed if change is to come. The truth is that mission, especially British and American mission, has almost always been done from a place of presumed white and/or British and/or American superiority. The missionary is invariably considered to be the giver and the ones being ministered to are the receivers. To continue to cover it up only prolongs abuse of the racialization of the cultural other.

Questions for Reflecting

1. What was behind the European hubris in the early days of the establishing of the colonies to make them think the land already belonged to them? Do a quick study on your electronic devices and report back concerning the doctrine of discovery.

2. As you go through America's missional history, the dehumanization of Indigenous people is common in the language used and actions taken. If missionaries can be excused by simply saying they were reflecting the attitudes of their own time, how would anything ever change? What of those few courageous missionaries in every era who stood up to the degrading attitudes in their own generation? How can both be "people of their time"? Who deserves more honor?

3. Prior to reading this chapter, did you know about residential Indian boarding schools and the abuses Indian children suffered? If so, how did you learn about this era? If not, why do you think you have not learned about it up to this point?

4. What is the "great missional cover-up"? Have you been a part of it? If yes, in what ways? If no, how did you avoid it?

Chapter Four

Missional Pedagogy

"The illiterate of the 21st century will not be those who cannot read and write, but those who cannot learn, unlearn, and relearn."—Alvin Toffler

In his book *Pedagogy of the Oppressed,* Paulo Freire speaks of the role of the teacher and student in his "banking" concept of education, which he posits is used to oppress the masses. Often, the oppression is unintentional, but through common pedagogical assumptions, oppression occurs just the same.

> In the banking concept of education knowledge is a gift bestowed by those who consider themselves knowledgeable, upon those who they consider to know nothing. Projecting an absolute ignorance onto others, a characteristic of the ideology of oppression, negates education and knowledge as process of inquiry. The teacher presents himself to his students as their necessary opposite; by considering their ignorance absolute, he justifies his own existence. The students, alienated like the slave in the Hegelian dialect, accept their ignorance as justifying the "teacher's" existence—but, unlike the slave, they never discover that they educate the teacher . . . The idea is that the narration (with the teacher as narrator) leads students to memorize mechanically, the narrated content. Worse yet, it turns them into "containers" or "receptacles" to be filled by the teacher. The more completely she fills the receptacles, the better a teacher she is. The more meekly the receptacles permit themselves to be filled, the better students they are.[1]

---

1. Freire, *Pedagogy of the Oppressed,* 53.

I have always considered pedagogy to be at least as important as content. In other words, what is caught is actually more impacting than what is taught. The presumed superiority of the missionary over the one being missionized, is, as I earlier suggested, an assumption simply "baked into the bread" of modern mission.

If we take the liberty to substitute the words *missionary* and *missionized* for Freire's use of *teacher* and *student* below, it may help to examine the heart of the epistemological assumptions common in most missionary endeavors.

a. The [missionary] teaches and the [missionized] are taught;

b. The [missionary] knows everything, and the [missionized] know nothing;

c. The [missionary] thinks and the [missionized] are thought about;

d. The [missionary] talks and the [missionized] listen—meekly;

e. The [missionary] disciplines and the [missionized] are disciplined;

f. The [missionary] chooses and enforces his choice and the [missionized] comply;

g. The [missionary] acts and the [missionized] have the illusion of acting through the action of the [missionary];

h. The [missionary] chooses the program content, and the [missionized] (who are not consulted) adapt to it;

i. The [missionary] confuses the authority of knowledge with his or her own professional authority, which she and he sets in opposition to the freedom of the [missionized];

j. The [missionary] is the subject of the learning process, while the [missionized] are mere objects.[2]

The conclusion to the Freire paradigm is that the teacher, or in our case, the missionary, regardless of their good intentions, is an agent of oppression to the student. As one who comes from a context of perhaps the most missionized people in America, I can say without hesitation, Christian mission has been, from the start of modern American history, a destructive and oppressing juggernaut among America's Indigenous people and around the world. The devastation that has occurred because of Christian

---

2. Freire, *Pedagogy of the Oppressed*, 54.

mission is not because missionaries are a horrible class of people or because they had bad intentions. The incalculable amount of damage done by Christian mission is because of the presumed superiority of one culture, who understood themselves as somehow better than the others, and felt they held absolute truth over the cultural other.

> What even 20th century Americans have clearly inherited from New England Puritans ... is a need to see themselves as divinely appointed users of the earth for the good of all mankind. ... Their [Puritan] distinguishing mark is their overriding belief in themselves as a community saved by God for a special purpose in the world.[3]

Hypocrisy from the Top

Perhaps it will be difficult for establishment churches and mission-sending agencies to accept this critique. After all, missionaries are considered the heroes of the Western church. Perhaps they personify what people want to believe are the best of human aspirations. Perhaps that's why missionaries are considered to be a sort of "protected class," especially those who, in the midst of American colonial genocide, we so revere, such as John Elliot or David Brainerd. The inclination to protect our missionaries' reputations was never more evident than when Pope Francis bestowed sainthood on Junipero Serra. Serra was first set on the track for sainthood by Pope John Paul II on September 28, 1988. That pope stated,

> He [Serra] sowed the seeds of Christian faith amid the momentous changes wrought by the arrival of European settlers in the New World. It was a field of missionary endeavor that required patience, perseverance, and humility, as well as vision and courage.[4]

The contrast between the hypocrisy of the church and the reality of those who were missionized could not be greater. Serra's cruelty to Indigenous people is well documented but in an open letter to Pope Francis, published by *The Huffington Post*, this tragedy and my sentiments concerning it are laid out for all to see.

Dear Pope Francis,

---

3. Segal and Stineback, *Puritans, Indians, and Manifest Destiny*, 224.
4. John Paul II, "Tribute."

While the rest of the country celebrates your voice for the poor and disenfranchised, I mourn your disregard for the most disenfranchised people in North America. While you are lauded for your concern over human rights, I wonder why your concern only goes to those most identified in America with Settler Colonialism? In speaking of immigration to US Congress, you said:

> Tragically, the rights of those who were here long before us were not always respected. For those people, and the nations, from the heart of American democracy, we affirm my highest esteem and appreciation. Those first contacts were often turbulent and violent, but we know it's very difficult to judge the past by the criteria of the present.

Then, wait for it . . . yes, the congress applauds.

Honourable Pope Francis, may I express to you the age-old lesson that history repeats itself? People and governments repeat the "sins and the errors of the past" by not fully dealing with their responsibilities in the past. Your casual reference to the sins of America's past, while never even naming our peoples as First Nations, Native Americans or Indigenous peoples, only helps to justify and reinforce to the body . . . which you addressed, our continued mistreatment and our relegation to their intentions for us to fade into quiet oblivion. Your references to Jesus' words to "do unto others as you would want them to do to you" feels to me like mere hypocrisy after such an affront to Indigenous peoples. To add to the pain, each congressional applause only inserted an exclamation point to your callousness to America's Indigenous plight and serve[d] to prop up their own justification in not dealing with America's genocidal past systemic record.

Your insistence on the canonization of Friar Junipero Serra was outrageous to Indigenous people everywhere but as we saw in your address to Congress, that heinous act simply reinforces your disregard for the rights of Indigenous peoples. Serra, a man responsible for most of the imprisonment and colonization of northern California's Indigenous peoples, is more than affront, it is an egregious sin. You, who speak so highly of the sanctity of life and the value of family, insisted on canonizing a man who ha[d] total disregard for the lives of those to whom he was "spreading the gospel." Serra allowed his men to rape Native women and kill their objectors. He tortured and maimed those who resisted his message of Christianity, and he kidnapped children only to be reunited with their parents after everyone agreed to family baptisms into Christianity and to perpetual enslavement. Hear Serra's own words:

> I would not feel sorry no matter what punishment they gave them, if they would commute it to prison for life, or in the stocks every day, since then it would be easier for them to die well. Do you think it possible that if they kept them prisoners for a time, and by means of interpreters explained to them about the life to come and its eternal duration, and if we prayed to God for them—might we not persuade them to repent and win them over to a better life? You could impress on them that the only reason they were still alive is because of our affection for them, and the trouble we took to save their lives.

Furthermore, Serra was officially justified in his actions because of the Catholic Doctrine of Conquest. Pope Francis, if you love justice, as God does, why not revoke the papal bulls of 1452 and 1493, collectively known as the "Doctrine of Discovery" which justified the cession of all lands "discovered" by "Christians" like Serra and, Columbus? These marching orders by the church gave authority to Catholics and influenced Protestants alike, to partake in carte blanche enslavement of Africans and Indigenous peoples everywhere and to justify worldwide land theft and genocide. But perhaps even genocide cannot be judged using today's standards according to your suggestion?

Which brings me to my final concern—your rationale. You say we can't judge the mistakes of the past by today's standards? But what about judging the sins of the past according to the legacy of brave men and women who have stood up for the rights of Indigenous peoples before, during and after Serra's, (and other church representatives') time? Why not judge them according[ly] to be godly persons of their own times? Your presumption disregards the long legacy of those whom I consider to be true heroes, who protested slavery, condemned forced missions and risked their lives to protest Indigenous people from land theft and murder. Your argument dishonours these historic and present prophetic voices. By your own rationale to disregard the sins of the past against Indigenous peoples, you dishonour the sacrifices those righteous heroes have made. Are we not to honour those who deserve honour?

Pope Francis, you are likely a wonderful person, but you apparently have little sense of justice when it comes to the marginalized and still disenfranchised Indigenous peoples of America. And, sadly to say, speaking only for myself, from where I stand, the Indigenous people of America, and those who have stood up for them in the past and present, are much closer to Jesus than you.[5]

I never received a response from the pope or the Vatican, or even a disgruntled bishop or priest. The point here is that Serra's sainthood status is similar to the hypocritical esteem Christians give to all their missionaries. The missionary status is considered by all in the mission enterprise to be sacrosanct, and beyond reproach. Yet, if we do not critique our own movements and our own people, we will surely be judged by history later. Change is difficult; systemic change even more difficult; and changing deep-seated myths is more difficult still. Perhaps by putting the problem in a biblical context, we can see that moving through such changes is nothing new, and even necessary for the good news to move forward.

Tribalism and Hospitality

What might be considered the negative side of tribalism is always in tension with extending hospitality to one's neighbors. Perhaps our most primordial intuitions are geared towards self-preservation. Contrary to the patterns of Western individualism, it took a whole group, usually in the form of a clan or a tribe, in order to survive the earliest of times. I am always in wonder at the difficulties faced by the television subjects of shows like *Alone, Dual Survival,* and *Naked and Afraid.* The idea of these particular reality television programs is for the contestants to use their primitive skills in order to survive like so called "primitive" humans once did. The problem with the proposition is that what they assume to be primitive individual persons, were actually complex societies in which each person understood their role through the lens of how it benefitted the survival of the whole group. Selfishness and individualized labour did not exist except as it came through banishment, the most severe form of punishment. I suppose a better name for these shows would be *Banishment.*

Even in Native American people's highly formed sense of tribalism, one of the most apparent values was hospitality to others and generosity to strangers. A person or small group that was experiencing a struggle surviving was often taken in by the tribe of the band or clan that found them, providing shelter and sustenance until they could continue on their journey.

5. Woodley, "Pope's Hypocritical Stance."

> On reading the various accounts and monographs by explorers and anthropologists, what strikes one is the almost universal hospitality shown by Indian tribes, especially to their White visitors. It is quite remarkable as described in David Bushnell's writings about explorers and missionaries among the Siouan, Algonquian, and Caddoan tribes west of the Mississippi . . . There are practically no examples of inhospitality or harsh treatment rendered to Whites. On the contrary, the tribal leaders went out of their way to receive these visitors as special guests. There seems to have been a conviction among the Indians, at least until the middle of the 19th century, that they and the newcomers could share the land equally, even if the land was sometimes thought to be the tribes' sacred inheritance.[6]

The Indigenous value of hospitality was very much in line with the biblical values of shalom. Not only was the ethic of hospitality/generosity a consistently stated value through the First Testament via what I call the "shalom-sabbath-Jubilee principle," it was the cornerstone on which Jesus drew for his life and teachings.

The tension between the tendency to protect one's own clan or tribe, or as we later experience, one's own "race," and treating the cultural other with the same dignity and equity as themselves, is resilient. This tension is evident in the stories of the Hebrew Bible. For example, the story of the conquest of Joshua into Canaan is almost diametrically opposed to the story of how Abraham enters the land. On the one hand, Joshua is a bloody warrior, smiting his enemies, including their women, children, and even their animals. On the other hand, Abraham enters the same land of Canaan, with the same promise given by God that was given to Joshua to inherit the land, and he is a perfect guest at every turn. Deciphering the tension between these two binary ideologies are the voluminous works of theologians and biblical scholars spanning the millennia. But in that tension one can understand why the Jews represented in the Second Testament are reluctant to allow the Gentiles to receive the good news about Jesus. Other glaring examples of the significance of hospitality include that of Sodom and Gomorrah and the story of Jonah's reluctance to assist the people of Nineveh.

The Jewish Rabbi Jesus appears on the scene of Second Temple Judaism declaring his message and himself to be representing the true intentions of the Jewish God, Yahweh. But to Jesus, Yahweh is not solely the God of Israel, Yahweh is God of the whole earth. Jesus' message concerning a

---

6. Starkloff, *People of the Center*, 88.

new reign of God is anchored in an ancient shalom-sabbath-Jubilee ethic, with which the people of his day were pervasively aware. Yet, Jesus presents this shalom realm of God as being something both old and new. He claims, in his mysteriously idiomatic stories and sayings, that they have missed the real heart of the Law and thereby are missing out on knowing God. He claims to have come not to destroy the Law, but rather to fulfill it. So far, so good.

The trouble comes when Jesus, in claiming to know the heart of Yahweh, includes not only those who are inside the obedience of the Law. He opens the door to those outside Judaism, in other words, to the cultural other. The non-exclusionary theme we often find in the Hebrew Bible, built on the ancient ethic of shalom, was how Jesus himself understood the Torah/Law. This is the same dilemma that his disciple Peter faced in his dealings with the Gentile, Cornelius. In fact, the most important decision made by the newly formed Jesus followers was the discussion in Acts 15 over whether or not to release the good news to the Gentiles. We do not know the exact content of those meetings, but surely Jesus' parables, sayings, words, and acts of nascent hospitality to the cultural other must have been much of the focus. The good news of the reign of God, they discovered, that was taught and lived by Jesus, had been God's intentions from the very beginning. Accepting the cultural other as an equal is the very heart of the gospel of Jesus Christ.

God Is Different, Different Is Good

When we examine the brilliant stars shining clearly against a darkened night sky or stand alone on an ocean beach seeing waves and water as far as the eye can see, it is easy to feel a sense of our own human insignificance. But if we look closer, we may discover we are not alone. There is a life principle at work within the whole community of creation. Everything is distinct from the other. No two snowflakes are exactly the same, nor leaves on a tree, nor creatures of the same species, nor fingerprints, retinal scans, voice patterns, and so on. Nothing that exists is exactly the same as anything else. This is God's great master plan of diversity. But at the same time, just then we might allow our diversity to be the driving force of the universe and come to wrong conclusions about the preeminence of individualism. At that point we also realize that nothing in creation is alone.

Nothing exists as a single, lonely entity in the whole community of creation. From the expansive multiverse down to the single human cell, joined to other cells, nothing is alone. We have a saying among our Indigenous people that translates to "all my relations." That prayer, if you will, covers the acknowledgment that we as human beings are related to everything else that exists and what we do affects everything else in some way. The prayer acknowledges both the things seen and the things hidden from view.

When I was in grade school, science teachers everywhere assumed the basic building blocks of all atomic matter to be protons, neutrons, and electrons. Since that time, particle theory has come a long way. In the mid-1960s physicists Murray Gell-Mann and George Zweig realized there was more to it, and they proposed a theoretical model of something more within the foundational building blocks of the universe. Their theory introduced the world to the possibility of something they called "quarks." Quarks are the building blocks of protons and neutrons and it even gets more complicated than that. Many scientists who have aided us in our understanding of the foundations of life have discovered that one of the most fascinating things about quarks is that they are never alone. They move around and appear to change their groupings and direction, but no solitary quark exists.

From the multiverse to quarks, everything that exists, exists within relationship to something else. And why should it be any different? The fingerprints on creation are not our own. The very DNA of everything seen and unseen is relational, in community with the other. The Creator, or God as many call the divine being, forms everything to be a reflection of God's own self. The Great Mystery has allowed us to see a reflection of its being through the design of creation. No one is alone, not even God.

God's Goodness, Enough for Everyone

Within the great balance of nature there exists another law that affects everything. Stronger forces are allowed to take over the weaker and yet we all do what we need in order to survive. This drive to survive is demonstrated well in the four-legged animal kingdom. Everyone has watched footage from nature shows as a fox runs down a rabbit or a pack of wolves take down a bison. The principle, as I understand it, is that something must die for others to live. In the animal world this is a means of survival. Notice, though, that the victor only kills what is needed to survive. People are different than animals in this regard.

Human animals are distinct from others in that they have been given a choice and the ingenuity to survive without killing each other. Empires are made not of necessity, but of choice. When living by the adage "only the strong survive," we actually make a moral choice as to who will be strong and who will be weak. Jesus turns this imperial impulse on its head, teaching that the weakest, most vulnerable among us should be protected, cared for, and even goes as far as saying they have the favor of God.

The ancient idea of caring for the widow, the orphan, and the immigrant is embedded deep within many religious communities. Jesus commanded his followers to care for the poor and the "least of these," teaching humanity a renewed view of how to live in a state of vulnerability. Jesus showed humanity how to use power, not to gain advantage over the vulnerable and marginalized, but rather to empower those who are disenfranchised, even to the point of viewing them as our teachers. The story of Jesus in the Scriptures is clear: we learn through our vulnerability. God must be the most vulnerable being in existence.

God comes to earth as a vulnerable and needy child. Not just a helpless baby, but born in the humblest of venues, a barn, in a hay trough, laid among mouse poop and camel spit. His parents are not wealthy and because of unjust laws they must become refugees. The child grows up, likely in his teenage years losing his father, becoming the child of a young single mother. He lives a lifestyle among the poor and broken and despised of an unjust society. Since Jesus has been afforded just a bit more privilege than some, he accepts them and welcomes them. He learns from those who are disenfranchised and he teaches others to do the same. Jesus becomes homeless but continues to make others aware of his insights. Eventually, he is set up by the authorities, jailed, beaten, and convicted of sedition. That child, who was born in a feed trough, as a man dies the death of a criminal even though his life's purpose was to bring justice to the world. The good news from God from the incarnation to the cross is vulnerability. Jesus demonstrated a life of vulnerability and he taught it throughout his life. The modern American mission era has, by and large, lived and taught the opposite.

Questions for Reflecting

1. In what ways have missionaries oppressed the cultural other simply by the way they have taught?
2. Do you consider my letter to the pope to be too critical? If so, in what ways? If not, in what ways were his address and actions hypocritical?
3. In what ways is church a positive form of tribalism? How could the church reflect God's natural passion for diversity?
4. How do you feel about the statement, "God must be the most vulnerable being in existence." How does that affect your thoughts and theologies about God?

PART 2

Considering New Missional Foundations

Chapter Five

Demographic Realities and Whiteness Theologies

> "Indigenolatfricasiana (Indigeno-latfri-casiana) Meaning: the increasing importance and influence of global Indigenous, Latin American, Africana, Asian, and the peoples of Oceana, and the descendants of these diverse people groups, in the declining Euro/American, Western-dominated world and worldview."—RANDY WOODLEY

WE KNOW THE WORLD around us is changing faster than ever and as a result cultures and even worldviews are changing as well. There are multitudes of books and articles addressing these realities, and the conditions that inspire the writings are changing exponentially. Undoubtedly, before this work has been published, the numbers and feelings about the changes in our culture will have intensified. Here are just a few general trends you should be aware of:

- In 2008 more than one-third of the people in the United States were Black or Indigenous and other People of Color (BIPOC)
- In 2013 over half of the all children born in the United States were BIPOC and this will only continue to increase
- In 2014 over half of all school children were BIPOC
- In 2042 over 50 percent of the people in the United States will be BIPOC

- The white population will continue to decline and eventually become the most recognizably and fastest declining minority in the United States[1]

The clear trend is what some call "the browning of America." The white race is declining, and BIPOC, or non-whites, are increasing. In a study of immigration trends and projections, covering a one-hundred-year period, 1965–2065, the Pew Research Center found that in the past fifty years, half of population growth can be attributed to immigrants coming to the US. Over the next fifty years that share is expected to rise to 88 percent, drastically changing the ethnic and racial makeup of the country.[2] At the same time, people in America are abandoning Christianity at an alarming rate. This trend is expected to continue while the rate of those who consider themselves religiously unaffiliated rises sharply. From 2007 to 2014 the religiously nonaffiliated or "nones" rose from around 36 million in 2007, to around 56 million in 2014. The cohort that most strongly identifies as being religiously unaffiliated is millennials.[3]

Indigenolatfricasiana is a word I somewhat humorously coined representing these trends and changes in the world, including the church. However, institutions such as the church have historically changed at a much slower rate that society in general. In part, this inability to change is one of the primary reasons I believe Christianity is declining in America, especially among younger people. The millennial generation and Gen Z have for the most part accepted the idea of a world without personal and structural racism. They find churches' inability to carry out such commands to "love thy neighbor" to be hypocritical. But I don't think the dominant white American church actually wants to change. I think the modern church is stuck in the American myth, which includes in it a denial of its own forms of white supremacy, and therefore, it won't change.

Receiving and Releasing the Gospel across Worldviews

I suppose all of us who follow Jesus have, or at one time had, deep within us a certain commonality—namely, a desire for change. Hopefully, the era of missional individualism will end soon—the idea where we think that if we

1. Buxton, "So You're About To Become A Minority . . ."
2. Pew Research, "Modern Immigration Wave."
3. Pew Research, "America's Changing Religious Landscape."

just change enough individuals in the system, the system will change. I like the instructions commonly attributed to Salvadoran martyr Archbishop Oscar Romero: "It is not enough to undertake works of charity to alleviate the suffering of the poor; we must transform the structures that create this suffering." Systemic thinking is not anti-individualistic; it is simply a wider view. So let's be honest. We really do want to change the world and that means changing, or influencing, if that feels less invasive, people, cultures, and worldviews of others and our own. This type of change comes through changing systems and structures.

The key to good missiology is not to avoid change, but rather to be honest about it and to be aware of our own cultural baggage, as well as our own worldview. We should ensure that we are not changing the world into our own image and our own machinations but rather, as best as we all can determine together, asking what are the desires of Jesus for that particular person, system, or cultural concern. Systemic change is needed in any system where shalom is broken. So, we must first ask ourselves, why has mission concentrated so much energy in the past on individual conversions, most often ignoring systems and structures?

Brazilian Archbishop Helder Camara said, "When I feed the hungry, they call me a saint. When I ask why they have no food, they call me a Communist."[4] It is true that the communist scare of the first half of the twentieth century had a deep influence on the political thinking of all Americans. The "Red Scare" also seeped into our education systems, our economic philosophies, and our religious landscape. Recently there has been a resurgence of that fear, dreading any sort of anti-individualism, such as the many forms of socialism, as being "born of communism." Ironically, the New Testament church operated much closer on the scale of socialism than it did capitalism.

In order to make changes in a culture we must examine the culture's roots, or perhaps even put more aptly, the cultural DNA. By looking back, we can sometimes discover a way forward, and also the deeper (and even the divine) purposes upon which a society was founded. North America, our continent, has been influenced by three strong cultures, Native American culture, made up of hundreds of individual tribes with many commonalities (and differences); African American culture (primarily post-slavery); and Euro-American culture, a social construction that combines most of the white tribes into one group. Other cultural contributions are extremely

4. Quoted in Dear, *Peace Behind Bars*, 65.

important as well, such as Latinx, Asian, and Jewish. The difference between these cultures exists in their ability, in the case of the Indigenous cultures, or inability, in the case of the white tribes, to negotiate difference. If we are going to tackle the evils of globalization and its resultant systems, we should first begin in our own backyard.

Race and Racism

There is but one race in the realm of humanity, namely the human race. In Acts 17:26 the apostle Paul states that "from one man, God made every nation." The word *nation* used here is *ethne'* in the Greek, from which we get the idea of ethnic groups. There are various ethnicities (all glorious) but only one race of humans, and all humanity comprise that one race. The idea of different races among humans (a fabricated, socially constructed reality) was a misguided, unscientific[5] attempt to classify people according to their physical characteristics. Ultimately, a pseudoscience called race theory became useful for *racists*, even though in reality we are all one race. The world of mission was not exempt from the influence of race theory.

Although race may not be a real thing, unfortunately *racism* is a verifiable reality. Even in our recent past American racists have used various forms of race theory to propagate white supremacy. Race theories like eugenics have been touted for over a century as science. Eugenics, popular in white European-influenced countries like the United States, South Africa, Australia, and England, influenced Hitler's master race theory resulting in the Holocaust of six million Jews, along with others thought by the Nazis to be genetically less desirable. This purported science was not based on fact but rather on notions of ethnic superiority. Fabricated realities such as "whiteness" were attempts to shift the base of power so people who looked like one another could control other people who looked different. The idea behind eugenics and its influence was, and still is, to assimilate all people with similar physical characteristics into one group or race. Generally, positive eugenics encouraged white people to have more children and to raise those who were not too different than themselves to the higher standard of the so-called "white race." Negative eugenics sought to discourage Black, Indigenous, and other people of color from having children, which among

---

5. Put succinctly, if we can interbreed, we are of the same race.

other atrocities, resulted in thousands of nonconsensual sterilizations, especially of Black and Indigenous women.[6]

Becoming White

One clear example of race assimilation into white America was the experience of the Irish. After centuries of English subjugation and years of forced monocultural food-crop servitude, growing potatoes for the English, Ireland experienced a potato blight. The English and Irish gentry responded by foreclosing on debts and evicting people from their homes, leaving many Irish penniless and homeless. Those Irish who were fortunate enough to make their way to America found a generally unwelcoming society awaiting them. Their hurdles included not just anti-Catholic sentiment, but, as Noel Ignatiev points out, they needed to "become white" in order to obtain the privileges afforded only to America's new social order, namely, those who could assimilate into the socially constructed category of "whiteness."[7]

The reality in America was that the white tribes (those with lighter hued skin color, especially from Western Europe) were creating a system of oppression that would automatically disenfranchise those who were physically and culturally different from them. The English, the Scottish, the French, the Belgians, the Germans, the Scandinavians, the Spanish, the Irish, the Eastern Europeans (including Jews), and the Italians would eventually trade in much of their old-world heritage and culture for a new white American identity. For everyone else—namely, Black, Indigenous, Latinx, and Asian people—the road would be much longer and full of roadblocks, making assimilation more difficult.

My analysis does not intend to diminish the difficulties that some groups of Europeans experienced upon their arrival. Nearly every group had initial periods of resistance from the rest of society. Thus, for many of the white ethnicities, the American success myth of "pull yourself up by your own bootstraps" became by necessity a lived reality. The problem with the American Dream is that we use the language and idea freely with the underlying assumption that it can be applied universally. Non-European peoples in America would find no mythological "bootstraps" because, too often, they were prevented from owning their own boots!

---

6. See Painter, *History of White People.*
7. Ignatiev, *How the Irish Became White.*

Central to the American dilemma, from the Pilgrims onward, was the fact that the white ethnicities experienced an identity crisis as well. What was the cost of becoming a white American for these immigrants? They gave up language, culture, and all that made them unique in the world for the high price of becoming "white." These immigrants were no longer English or Dutch or Spanish, yet they were living, as far as they, and their kings were concerned, on the soil of the country laying claim to that portion of America. The English newcomers strangely found themselves in *New* England, the Dutch in *New* Amsterdam or the Spanish in *New* Spain. Ignoring the Indigenous people's claims to the land from time immemorial, the Europeans needed to find a "civilized" and seemingly "just" claim to the land. As a result, false theologies of divine favor, illegitimate legacies of unauthorized land claims, and dishonest myths of the "American savages" were propagated to justify the theft of land from America's host peoples.

For example, the Puritans' need for a real identity was strained until they filled the missing gap in their myth, seeing themselves as "spiritual Israel," which they felt granted them a divinely favored place within Christianity. The Puritans had a whole colony/continent to develop along that theme. In what appeared to be endless land, only the Native American tribes stood between them and future generations of white prosperity. Although precarious at times, a newfound freedom of thought was strangely strengthened as the Pilgrims realized they were out of reach from kings and Old-World magistrates. In the "New World" the Pilgrims' loyalty to old alliances faded. New opportunities arose. But the best they could imagine at first was a "New England," so they forged a new identity founded predominately on their old familiar constraints. Missing the obvious, they settled for an American identity that deliberately neglected input from the Indigenous inhabitants of the land and from the land itself, thereby ignoring God's imprint on the land and its host people. This imprint included past revelations and God's active presence that would have connected all those components into an understanding of a very real American identity.

Avoiding Replacement Theologies

Theologians have argued for millennia over how much about God a person can know by observing creation. The question ultimately boils down to the idea that some theologians, who approach the subject from a redemption-based theology, believe the human heart to be so darkened by sin that people cannot have a real knowledge of God from creation. Other theologians believe that creation is a witness of the truth, able to lead one to a knowledge of God that is testified to in the Scriptures. I believe the latter to be true. This creation-based theological premise is also basic to most, if not all, Native American belief systems.

With the Protestant Reformation came a strong emphasis on a redemption-based theology, coupled later with an Enlightenment worldview. This view stacked the deck against a wider view of revelation and the narrower view became the standard in most theological circles. Since Indigenous people's views of Creator are based almost wholly on God's ability to communicate with us, both directly and through nature, there was little tolerance for other views. The theological basis for a redemption-based view continued to be dominant during the heaviest years of modern mission.

I understand truth to be universal and readily available to everyone. This means that everyone should be able to apply universal revelation, at least to some degree, to themselves. Those people subjected to modern missions were not given the opportunity to apply their own theologies to themselves, in part because a redemption-based emphasis in Christianity limits the ability for God to speak to all people. Most of the early missionaries did not believe that God had spoken to non-Western peoples prior to the arrival of Europeans. To them, this meant that the people they were trying to reach with the gospel had no stories they considered worth hearing. In most cases, they did not want to hear about other people's stories that expressed a relationship with the Creator for millennia. The result was that the missionaries believed the only stories worth telling were their own stories of Christ, contextualized to their own European cultural and theological standards. Non-Western peoples' theologies were considered pagan or demonic at worst, and childlike at best, needing to be replaced with a European, redemption-based theology.

As far as I have been able to determine, Indigenous people have always had an emphasis on a creation-based theology. Perhaps how far a group travels from their Indigenous roots towards modernization is directly related to their willingness to do theology from a creation-based approach. A loss of connection with the land and the understanding of this connection as the means of how directly the Creator can speak to us, and even intervene in our lives, may contribute greatly to a loss of a creation-based theology.

Since the theological emphasis of a redemption-based approach is founded on the ideas of guilt and sin, the natural result is a negative view of culture and creation. A creation-based theology lends itself to a more positive, or at least a neutral, view of culture and a high view of creation. I believe all cultures, at least in part, are divinely constructed and reflect God or point to God, by either denying or accepting truth. These truths, or the denial of them, are expressed in the lifestyle, language, traditions, ceremonies, and stories of the people. In other words, God is revealed within culture. In this sense culture is a God-given gift that should be considered as part of creation. A creation-based approach to theology therefore attends to the importance of culture.

On the other hand, if a redemption-based approach is the primary theology, then culture is usually viewed as sin-stained or even evil. Therefore any culture is able to be replaced, or as some would say "redeemed," by another culture that is thought to be more "Christian." Because most of the Reformers placed the emphasis on redemption and the fallen nature of human beings, they felt that they could justify replacing other cultures with their own so-called "Christian culture."

According to Stephen Bevans, a redemptive-based approach "is characterized by the conviction that culture and human experience are either in need of a radical transformation or in need of total replacement."[8] The modern evangelical church has by and large adopted a redemption-based theology while rejecting a creation-based theology. This focus ordinarily emphasizes the sinfulness and inadequacy of human beings and their cultures. The answer to their dilemma is the power of the cross of Christ. This view is not completely incorrect in that we are all limited by our humanity.

But, human beings are not bound to be helpless nor ineffective in cooperating with the Creator in the process of their own healing/salvation. Our cooperative efforts lead us to discover the Creator in creation, in our own cultures, in each other, in the marginal places of society. A creation-based theological approach can find truth and ultimately God in these places because life is good, creation is good, and the Creator can be found in all truth.

The good news from Jesus says both "yes" and "no" to every culture but considers cultural context to be of extreme importance. For Indigenous people, a redemption-based emphasis in theology has served to discredit our own theological stories of the God working among us in the past. This

---

8. Bevans, *Models of Contextual Theology*, 21.

approach has nullified the values we hold dear concerning egalitarianism and a strong sense of local community and has replaced them with hierarchy and individualism. Replacement theologies have stripped from Indigenous people worldwide the importance of a theology of the land and have replaced it with European-based contexts that objectify the land rather than treat it as a relative. If we are to take cultural contextualization seriously, it behooves us to understand how the colonizer has stripped Indigenous people of their natural birthright by limiting them to a redemption-based approach to the gospel.

Doing theology on a contextually local level implies that there is need for authentic relationship in the community. By ignoring the importance of place, one could make the mistake of developing a supposed "non-contextual theology." This is actually what occurred in the case of mission to North American Natives, Africans, and others. The missionary colonizers attempted to apply their own local European theology universally to the indigenous cultural context, and then called it "biblical truth," when in fact, it was truth to them in their European contexts only. Perhaps the influence of a redemption-based approach by missionaries can help to explain why so few Indigenous people are actually Christians. To approach Christian theology in a way that seems unnatural—Native Americans and others only stood to lose their own culture and values in the process.

For an example, consider the amount of control exercised in the typical modern church. Indigenous people have different values concerning control than do Euro-Americans. The concept of time is relevant in this example as well. In the modern church one must be on time, be seated in a particular place (staring at the back of someone's head), allow only the preacher to talk, stand up when given the cue, sit down when told, and stay seated during the message. To those from Native American cultures who view control as evil, and even as a form of witchcraft, a tightly controlled atmosphere such as this disturbs one's sense of spirituality.

One's worldview is paramount to understanding one's theology. In fact, the difference between a redemption and creation-based approach to theology has more to do with epistemology (how we come to know things), than it does with what is actually developed from Scripture study and revelation (or lack thereof). Worldviews come *a priori* but theology is developed. An interesting phenomenon has occurred among Native American Christians. While they may retain an Indigenous, non-Western worldview in many areas of life, they have actually adopted a theology based on a

Western worldview. This split in reality is understandable, given the particular history of Native American missions, but it causes considerable cognitive dissonance in the minds of Native American Christians.

The Native American Imprint

I find that most people from the white ethnic tribes are still somewhat uninformed concerning their connection to their own relationship with a Native American heritage. Understanding Native Americans may seem like a simple and familiar journey but I assure you that with over five hundred years of widespread misunderstandings, it will not be an easy corrective. I agree with President John F. Kennedy, who said,

> For a subject worked and reworked so often in novels, motion pictures, and television, American Indians remain probably the least understood and most misunderstood Americans of us all.

Kennedy went on to say,

> When we forget great contributors to our American history—when we neglect the heroic past of the American Indian—we thereby weaken our own heritage. We need to remember the contributions our forefathers found here and from which they borrowed liberally.... Before we can set out on the road to success, we have to know where we are going, and before we can know that we must determine where we have been in the past. It seems a basic requirement to study the history of our Indian people. America has much to learn about the heritage of our American Indians.[9]

John Kennedy was beginning to understand something that escapes most other Americans. America's history did not begin when Columbus or the Pilgrims arrival. While many Indigenous people believe they have always been here, others posit that our shared history began at least 27,000 years ago when small waves of immigrants found their way by land and sea from many directions to what America's Indigenous peoples call Turtle Island. Native Americans are part of America as much or more than any other group and yet most other Americans, regardless of when their ancestors arrived, are content to call First Nations history "their history" and European history "our history." I believe there are several reasons for this disclaimer by white Americans, the primary reason being a lack of a sense

9. Introduction to Josephy, ed., *American Indian*.

of land as theological place. Another reason preventing Euro-Americans from "buying in" to seeing themselves as a part of pre-"discovery" history involves the dismissal of Native American influence on the greater American society.

Philip Jenkins, in his *Dream Catchers: How Mainstream America Discovered Native Spirituality*, fills in much of the background concerning how historic American spirituality was influenced and formulated in relationship to America's First Nations. Jenkins deals with the ability of American society to steal spirituality from First Nations, capture it authoritatively (often supposedly becoming more of an authority than the native), and then note that the native is left as being seen in the position of the "helpless child" or the "ignorant savage." In this view, though admired, natives still remain "inferior" to the white man. Jenkins demonstrates how Native Americans can be admired while the old attitudes of superiority remain intact. The core of the book's content can be summed up in the following quote:

> Though the romanticized, environmentally sensitive Indians of *Dances with Wolves* or *Pocahontas* are much more attractive figures than the primitive savages of Victorian fantasy, their ideas and actions are still presented according to the taste of the mainstream non-Native audience, and are not necessarily any closer to any objective reality. The newer image may constitute a socially positive stereotype, but it is still a stereotype, defined according to non-Native and specifically Euro-American interests. While it is a much more benevolent dream, it is, nonetheless, a dream, shaped by its consumers, the dream catchers.[10]

The attitudes of European Americans were informed by myths portraying Indians as devil worshippers, savages, and uncivilized pagans. Typically, the Native Americans' supposed low spiritual state justified wars against them. Based on a superior moral claim, Euro-Americans also carried the responsibility of implementing various civilization policies such as forced, military-styled residential boarding schools.

Jenkins points out that after the Indians became somewhat "tamed" there began to develop a fascination from anthropologists and tourists, who were interested in native crafts. Following the curiosity phenomenon, romantic notions of Native Americans and myths of their spirituality came to be held more in admiration. Jenkins makes the case that the early twentieth

---

10. Jenkins, *Dream Catchers*, 19.

century was a particularly important period of change in many Americans' attitudes towards natives.

Because of its deep influence and because justice demands it, Americans, including the American church, need to face their own unscrupulous dealings with Native American spirituality. This is important because of the potential, but necessary, embarrassment that most Americans may have in admitting that Native Americans have had an influence, albeit a mythical influence, on the political, religious, and social landscape of the historical formation of America. This crack in the dyke can possibly open the door (in an age of pluralism) to allow the true Native voice to be one with historic authority.

And on the world front, we must ask, "What happened to the great missionary sending empire of 'the West to the rest?'" Yesterday's massive missionary enterprise is fast being replaced by what we can call, ethnically, the "browning of missions." The new paradigm of missions, as stated by Samuel Escobar in his *The New Global Mission*, is now from everywhere to everywhere and from everyone to everyone. We must all take stock, face reality, and ask ourselves hard questions such as, "Was Jesus really present in the Western mission-sending church of the twentieth century or were they simply a form of theologically and socially paternalistic white supremacy, feigning superiority and hegemony?" The answer is likely "yes" to both questions. But what of authority? How should we understand the way of Jesus except through "the book"? God has given us at least four "books," if you will, from which to guide our lifestyle and mission.

Questions for Reflecting

1. Why do you think the church is so slow to change? Do you hold any hope that this sluggish pattern could vary in the future? What gives you hope?

2. What does it mean for ethnic groups to become "white" in America?

3. Explain what a "replacement theology" is. What are some differences between a redemption-based view and a creation-based view?

4. Do you think Native Americans might have things to teach the church? Why or why not? Explain your answer.

Chapter Six

Negotiating God's "Four Books" and Questions of Authority

> "We all live inside the terrible engine of authority, and it grinds and shrieks and burns so that no one will say: lines on maps are silly."
> —Catherynne M. Valente

God's First "Book," Creation

CREATION IS GOD'S GIFT to us as a first teacher and she is a teacher for life. Although God may be an abstraction to us, in spite of all or efforts to make God concrete through theology, story, ceremony, and song, creation is the one solid, concretized demonstration where God exists. God embodies the wonders of sunrise to sunset each day. God shows God's self in the rainbow, the song of the loon, and the dance of the sage grouse. God's presence is there in the birth of every living creature and again in its death. And God is revealed throughout the life of every single cell and every complex system on earth and beyond.

Each of us, along with all living creatures, encounters creation before we can read or understand ideas about religion. Shared by all, that primordial sense of coming to grips with our earthly context is humanity's deepest spirituality. The earth is our first, most consistent, and most continuous teacher. The apostle Paul, having an understanding of Greek philosophy and various understandings of epistemological viewpoints, said it like this in Romans 1:19–20:

> They know the truth about God because he has made it obvious to them. For ever since the world was created, people have seen the earth and sky. Through everything God made, they can clearly see his invisible qualities—his eternal power and divine nature. So, they have no excuse for not knowing God.

The psalmist resounds in God's glory expressed via the earth throughout the Psalms, as in Psalm 19:1, "The heavens proclaim the glory of God. The skies display his craftsmanship." In Job 12:7–8 we read, "Just ask the animals, and they will teach you. Ask the birds of the sky, and they will tell you. Speak to the earth, and it will instruct you. Let the fish in the sea speak to you." Ecclesiastes and Proverbs extol the virtues of living close to nature and following the animal, insect, and all other creatures' habits. God has given us all dear Mother Nature, Mother Earth, as an ever-present guide and as a constant reassurance that God is nearby.

The earth is common to us all. Every creature, in the whole community of creation, including human creatures, has a common experience of living on earth. We all experience night and day and are in fact a part of each other's world and the systems that make up each day and year and lifetime. But nature can be unforgiving.

If God is revealed in creation, we would do well to ask, is God in the flood, the tornado, or the forest fire? Does God inhabit the hurricane, the severe drought, and the climate crisis? And while many of the disasters we are experiencing are created by human abuse, neglect, and violence, creating an imbalance to a world meant for harmony, real natural disasters do occur. Mirroring the story of Job, we ask his question: Do we experience God in the whirlwind? What Job was really asking of God was, why do good people suffer, or why is there suffering in the world? And for our particular discussion, why is there suffering in nature?

The question presumes God is responsible for these disasters, and therefore leads us to the conclusion that God is responsible for suffering. In the book of Job God's response to Job is to challenge his theological thinking. God's response is a correction of sorts to Job's inability to see the bigger picture.

> Where were you when I laid the earth's foundation?
>   Tell me, if you understand.
> Who marked off its dimensions? Surely you know!
>   Who stretched a measuring line across it?
> On what were its footings set,

>   or who laid its cornerstone—
> while the morning stars sang together
>   and all the angels shouted for joy?
> "Who shut up the sea behind doors
>   when it burst forth from the womb,
> when I made the clouds its garment
>   and wrapped it in thick darkness,
> when I fixed limits for it
>   and set its doors and bars in place,
> when I said, "This far you may come and no farther;
>   here is where your proud waves halt"?
> Have you ever given orders to the morning,
>   or shown the dawn its place,
> that it might take the earth by the edges
>   and shake the wicked out of it?
> The earth takes shape like clay under a seal;
>   its features stand out like those of a garment.
> The wicked are denied their light,
>   and their upraised arm is broken.
> Have you journeyed to the springs of the sea
>   or walked in the recesses of the deep?
> Have the gates of death been shown to you?
>   Have you seen the gates of the deepest darkness?
> Have you comprehended the vast expanses of the earth?
>   Tell me, if you know all this. (Job 38:4–18)

In this story, and for the remainder of the book of Job, God does not answer Job's question about suffering directly. Our human tendency is to blame God for the things we don't understand. Is it possible that God can be an ever-present inhabitation of creation and not be in control of it? Could the answer be a simple as the analogy of us and our children? They are born and we nurture them along as best we can but, in the end, they make their own choices based on nature, nurture, and something we call free will. Natural disasters disrupt our plans, our crops, our homes, and sometimes our lives but they also bring about renewal. For instance, some plants will not germinate except through extreme heat as in a wildfire. Flooding does often create a generative silt that naturally fertilizes the soil. In fact, all our Cherokee crops were planted in flood plains along rivers and creeks for this very reason. If we understand some of the disruptive cycles that seem to occur naturally on the land, they can produce some good. But what good is there in a tornado?

Perhaps the terrible disruptions in nature provide us with a deep sense of appreciation for the intended harmony and beauty in nature. There is a balance that we must always keep in mind when dealing with creation to meet our own human needs. That balance must be rooted in deep respect for every other creature on the land. It is sometimes difficult for us humans to remember that we share the land and sea and rivers and mountains with other creatures. Those creatures, large and small, have a claim to the same space as us, or at least a similar space nearby. And, because no place on earth seems to be exempt from these disruptions there is a commonality of human experience that we can all relate to, and come to one another's aid and even their defense if we can plan ahead. In Psalm 65:5–13 the writer expresses a number of emotions in his wonderment and praise of God.

> You faithfully answer our prayers with awesome deeds,
>   O God our savior.
> You are the hope of everyone on earth,
>   even those who sail on distant seas.
> You formed the mountains by your power
>   and armed yourself with mighty strength.
> You quieted the raging oceans
>   with their pounding waves
>   and silenced the shouting of the nations.
> Those who live at the ends of the earth
>   stand in awe of your wonders.
> From where the sun rises to where it sets,
>   you inspire shouts of joy.
> You take care of the earth and water it,
>   making it rich and fertile.
> The river of God has plenty of water;
>   it provides a bountiful harvest of grain,
>   for you have ordered it so.
> You drench the plowed ground with rain,
>   melting the clods and leveling the ridges.
> You soften the earth with showers
>   and bless its abundant crops.
> You crown the year with a bountiful harvest;
>   even the hard pathways overflow with abundance.
> The grasslands of the wilderness become a lush pasture,
>   and the hillsides blossom with joy.
> The meadows are clothed with flocks of sheep,
>   and the valleys are carpeted with grain.
>   They all shout and sing for joy!

Negotiating God's "Four Books" and Questions of Authority

First of all, the psalmist is recognizing that the God who created the world—including "the distant seas," "the mountains," and "the oceans"—is the same God recognized by all people everywhere. The universal God of all peoples is illuminated with phrases like, "You are the hope of everyone on earth, even those who sail on distant seas," "and silenced the shouting of nations," and "Those who live at the ends of the earth stand in awe of your wonders. From where the sun rises to where it sets, you inspire shouts of joy." The psalmist understands, by virtue of nature herself, that the scope of the Creator is beyond any one particular nation or religion but is as wide as the earth and heavens can be.

Isn't this the first lesson of creation? Amazement, wonderment, excitement, and awe are all mixed together into an inexpressible feeling of the acknowledgment that there is a force that exists much greater than we can even imagine. And imagining what or who that force actually is becomes the task of religion, science, and philosophy. Spirituality is therefore how we respond to that sense of awe and to our various findings. I am fortunate enough, during some parts of the year, to be able to see both the sunrise and sunset from my living room and from my back porch. My wife and I enjoy these inexpressible moments when the sun greets the day and when it takes its daily leave. No two sunrises or sunsets are the same because of barometric pressure, cloud formation, or the ever-changing position of the sun's course. Yet, we know what has been set in daily motion is far beyond our human skill set, experience, and aptitude.

I notice when I walk in woods that I experience one of two things. I am either noticing some form of order and repetition in the variety and spacing of trees, which lets me know that forest was replanted by humans at some point, or I notice a wide array of diverse trees and plants in no apparent order except diversity. If I find ordered trees with an apparent pattern, I understand that place was ordered or controlled by human engineering. However, in the diversity, what we humans sometimes misunderstand as chaos, I know that force, whether you believe the force is nature or God or something in between, is responsible; and that is most often the thing that awes me in a way expressed by the psalmist in Psalm 65. But the psalmist continues after making the various proclamations of God's universality.

With phrases like, "You take care of the earth and water it, making it rich and fertile," and "The river of God has plenty of water; it provides a bountiful harvest of grain," the rest of Psalm 65 speaks directly to the extreme abundance God intends to provide through God's constant presence and relationship with the earth. Creator has not abandoned the land but seeks to bless with the fullness it can produce. While it is true that thoughts of the land providing meadows "clothed with flocks of sheep" and valleys "carpeted with grain" are both symbols of economic prosperity and food security, it shows that human involvement in the process, when treating the land with respect, often meets human needs and even produces abundance. But to bend nature to meet human need is not to break it. And to utilize nature's bounty is not the same as to say creation exists solely for humanity. We must share it with all God's creatures, the whole community of creation, from the largest mammals to the smallest microbiotic organisms in the sea and soil, each equally important in our relationship to the earth. When it comes to producing abundance, we must respect the whole community of creation and the harmony that exists, or that at least existed at one time. We must bring about harmony in order to live in prosperity and security with the land.

The balance and beauty and harmony we see in nature reveals a beautiful Creator. The natural disruptions, even the cycle of death, reminds us that life is short and should be experienced as harmoniously as possible. Death and suffering are a constant reminder that life is for living well, and they point to a better way. Perhaps death and suffering are the gift of pointing us to living life well while we have the opportunity. Perhaps the comfort of God's presence is the greatest theological principle we can draw from theodicy.

I have observed that most of us feel a deep and primal desire to experience nature, but also to safeguard ourselves from the harsh realities of nature. This balance has been the plight of humanity from time immemorial. Despite our fear of the natural world, our constant captivation by the beauty of creation and all her creatures never ceases. If Jesus is an example of how we might view creation, we cannot neglect the stories that reveal his deep wonderment.

Jesus, in his ecological context, apparently had a relationship with trees, flowers, animals, birds, and fish. He spoke of foxes' homes, of the sparrow's place of importance in God's eyes, of the beauty of flowers. Jesus knew when grain was ready for harvest, he knew where to catch fish, he understood the weather, he knew when a tree was healthy or not and apparently observed the habits of a particular donkey. The Second Testament is filled with examples that speak of Jesus' connection to, and relationship with, nature. And, as the story goes, there were plenty of animals present to witness his birth. Jesus himself learned from creation. Might we not also follow in his lead?

Perhaps his "backwater" Galilean upbringing shielded Jesus from urban enticements, but even more, then, should we expect a country boy in the city to gander and gawk at the many huge buildings, and Roman chariots, to wonder about aqueducts and iron weaponry. Yet these were not Jesus' distractions. If he was distracted by anything, it was the wonderment of what he observed in creation. True to the Scriptures of his Jewish faith, he allowed these wonders to point him to the glories underneath his feet and surrounding him. Creation, for Jesus, and all Indigenous people, those who live close to the earth, is the greatest teacher. This fact does not take away the sanctity of the Scriptures but rather allows them to point to God's greatest gift to all humanity, and the whole community of creation, from time immemorial.

God's Second "Book," Conscience

Conscience is that ever-present, sometime nagging feeling compelling us all to do the right thing. To turn again to Paul's Letter to the Romans, in 2:15 he states, "They [the Gentiles] demonstrate that God's law is written in their hearts, for their own conscience and thoughts either accuse them or tell them they are doing right." In speaking of the Gentiles, who did not have the gift of the Law, Paul says, they had their conscience, which was a law in and of itself. All people know that they don't want someone to abuse them and therefore they should not abuse others. If they do, their conscience will let them know about it. We all know we would like to have enough food to eat and to have a good place to lay our heads. When we hear of others who are going without those needs being met, it is our conscience that pricks our hearts and says that we must do something about it.

Besides wanting the best for others because it's what we want for ourselves, I believe any fool can look at nature, human or otherwise, and deduce there is a design. We may argue robustly about how that design came to be, but even the simplest systems are too complex to be haphazard. Where there is a design, there is a Designer. I am thankful that the design in nature came with a counterpart in humanity in which we can judge what is right and what is not. Apparently as we go through life, in the words of Jiminy Cricket, our conscience should be our guide.

Our values tell us what we believe to be right and ethical, but our conscience tells us how to judge whether rightness or wrongness is being done. If life were a baseball game, our conscience would be the umpire. Once our values are set, our conscience decides where and if those values are being upheld. The values, or the rules of the game, can change over time. I have noticed peoples' conscience sometimes have a long ways to catch up to their values. I think the system also works conversely. When we violate our conscience enough, our values begin to change. The apostle Paul referred to this process as a "conscience seared with a hot iron." Apparently violating one's conscience enough, the pain of hypocrisy, will eventually bring about what sounds like a very unpleasant experience, leaving us scarred.

God's Third "Book," Community

Conscience isn't the only umpire in the game. John Donne's words echo throughout history: "No man is an island." In spite of the fact that America is likely the most individualistic society in history to share the earth, we cannot escape the values and mores established in our hearts and minds through the influence of our human community. People are naturally observant. We watch one another throughout the day and we think about the actions of those around us. We are exposed immediately to human community, watching parents go to work and come home, observing the actions of our caregivers, building and losing trust in our siblings and fellow human beings. We are, to a large degree, a product of our communal environment. As we grow older, we begin to come in contact with those who think like us in various areas or differently than us. We join groups, clubs, religions, and are eventually kneaded like the ingredients in bread, into understanding concepts like patriotism and other kinds of loyalties to those people, groups, and social ethics that formed us, and those that we rejected. No one is an island.

Just as we are influenced by others, we also influence others in one way or another. We make and miss connections throughout our entire lives and those connections or lack thereof teach others about who we are and how we understand ourselves. Like it or not, we are all role models for good, bad, or indifferent. Perhaps we don't even notice the fact that we are role models. Even if an individual feels as if they aren't influencing anyone, they are a role model to themselves, and thus, we enter the category of conscience once again—negotiating between the ideas and values that have influenced us and to what standards we are willing to hold ourselves. Within the world of self-mediation, we find ourselves with ease of conscience or pain of conscience, with integrity or hypocrisy. Blame the dilemma, at least in part, on the influence of community.

In the pre-modern worldview, community was much larger, including the Creator, the Great Mystery or Force behind all creation. Animals, birds, insects, plants, and trees all were a part of one's community. Like human role models, each had an influence on one's thinking and Creator was somehow behind it all. Like human community, certain other creatures were there to guide one through one's formation of community and personal values. Modernity has lost a large part of values formation simply by shutting out nature, and perhaps therefore shutting out Creator-God. When our actions primarily occur only among humans and the products made by human hands, when our thought process includes only a small aspect of community, we limit God and overestimate the value of solely human interaction.

I had a very good friend named Stan. Stan was a Quaker pastor with whom I met monthly for coffee. We had very honest conversations and the man was just a delight to be around. I had been teaching part-time at a Friend's (Quaker) Seminary and eventually, my family and I lived in the house Stan's Quaker meeting had built to help families like ours struggling financially. By this time we were not normal churchgoers, but we felt a sense of loyalty to the Friends and attended their church services for a few years. The Quakers have a programmed meeting much like any other church service, which we attended, and an unprogrammed meeting. The unprogrammed meeting is the one where they all sit, mostly in silence, for an hour or so, until someone feels led by the Spirit to make a remark. Stan really enjoyed the silent meetings. I didn't.

To be fair, I attended an unprogrammed meeting only once, but it just did not sit right with me. I struggled to find out why. It wasn't that silence was uncomfortable as much as it was on me needing to hear from Creator from a dank room with no windows, and only humans surrounding me. I know God can speak to people anywhere, even in the darkest and most lonely places, but my concern, at least for myself, was, why create such limited circumstances for God to speak through? God speaks to me through nature, showing God's insight through birds and trees and weather, and sometimes people. I have nothing against Quaker silent meetings, in fact, I have met many wonderful Friends who really enjoy that special time each week. But I told Stan I would gladly meet in the unprogrammed worship whenever they decided to meet outdoors. Unfortunately, that never happened.

God's Fourth "Book," the Scriptures

Speaking of Quakers, in 1652, a Baptist minister, Richard Stookes, spoke to George Fox, often referenced as the founder of Quakerism, telling him that the Bible he was showing him was the "Word of God." Fox replied that it was not so, it "was the words of God" not "God the Word," and told him that he understood the Scriptures to themselves say that they were the words of God, but Christ was the Word.[1] The following year, when answering a question in court, Fox again declared that "God was the Word and the Scriptures were writings." The Word had existed before the writings and had fulfilled them. If Jesus is the Word and the Scriptures only reflect him, how did the writings become sacrosanct?

In developed systems, such as Western Christian theology, that are embedded in Platonic dualism, the ethereal, such as thought and spirit, become privileged over actions and embodiment. As a result, the products of sacred thought are enshrined as sacrosanct. The Bible, a product of hundreds of years of church councils, has to Western Christians become elevated to a status never intended by most of its authors, or by Jesus. Consider his words to the Pharisees in Matthew 23:22–24, "What sorrow awaits you teachers of religious law and you Pharisees. Hypocrites! For you are careful to tithe even the tiniest income from your herb gardens, but you ignore the more important aspects of the law—justice, mercy, and faith. You should tithe, yes, but do not neglect the more important things. Blind guides! You strain your water so you won't accidentally swallow a gnat, but you swallow a camel!"

In the story, Jesus is not rejecting the Scriptures but a certain interpretation and application of them. In other words, the problem is not the writings themselves but how we approach them. Jesus called those particular Pharisees "hypocrites" and "blind guides" because of their views. Anytime we use the Scriptures to justify actions such as exclusion and hegemony, inconsistent with the greater principles of justice and mercy, we have elevated Scripture to do more harm than good, falling into the same blindness and hypocrisy that Jesus condemned. In the West, we fail to realize the extent of

---

1. Dobbs, *Authority and the Early Quakers*, 68.

the effect that a warped Greek philosophy has had on our society and how much Christianity has been influenced by that philosophy.

Platonic dualism was born over three thousand years ago in ancient Greece. The Greek philosopher Plato split reality in two, placing a higher degree of importance on the ethereal, abstract, nonmaterial world and a lesser degree of importance on the material world. Another famous philosopher, Aristotle, was a student of Plato. Aristotle is sometimes referred to as the originator of whiteness. He imagined certain races to be more valuable than others—and, of course, the lighter-hued peoples, such as himself and his people, were considered by him to be the most superior form of civilization know to humankind. Plato's influence on Aristotle was apparent; once we divide reality into greater and lesser, everything can be seen in hierarchies. Aristotle saw people like himself of greater value than those who were seemingly different from him. I will speak to this problem more directly in the next chapter.

In a divided reality, binary thinking becomes natural and whole worldviews develop that reason not holistically but in divided reality binaries, including assigning more value to one nation, tribe, race, or ethnos than another. In such a system, humans can be valued over the earth and the whole community of creation, placing humankind's needs above all others, forgetting we are all in a related system of reality of symbiosis and reciprocity, co-sustaining each other. False categories are created, such as plants and weeds, animals and varmints, even males as having more value than females.

This stream of dualism became a natural part of Western systems of "progress." And following the Enlightenment influences such as Descartes's belief that he was a soul but had a body, American systems inherited and embraced a false separation of a whole reality, which included Western Christianity. In the Western worldview, a wide gap exists between what one believes and what one actually does, even to the extent that one's correct beliefs equals action in the Western mind. The result for many Christians has been a disembodied theology that looks nothing like the teachings of Jesus.

Although Hellenistic influence can be found in the New Testament, Jesus does not appear to be terribly affected by it. Perhaps his rural Galilean childhood kept his more Hebraic and holistic worldview intact. A number of early church fathers, however, were affected by Greek dualisms and hierarchies. Some of them, such as Augustine, had an undue amount of influence.

Later, as we have seen, ethnocentric notions of white supremacy surfaced directly in pseudosciences such as race theory, craniology, and the modern eugenics movement. The array of false racialized theories was used to justify Native American genocide and African American enslavement. The false science of eugenics had a direct influence on Hitler's Jewish extermination plan, on tens of thousands of forced sterilizations of Black, Indigenous, and other women of color in America, and on the infamous Tuskegee experiments that allowed Black farmers with syphilis to believe they were being treated while they were simply used as untreated guinea pigs to determine the negative effects of the disease. Craniology, in the late nineteenth and early twentieth centuries, resulted in tens of thousands of Native American heads being severed from dead Indigenous bodies and shipped to museums such as the Smithsonian, where many of them remain today.

When Western society wanted to use these now-debunked theories of Western science and the roots from whence they were derived for economic gain, it used blood quantum to do so. African Americans could be enslaved as free labor with only one drop of African blood, whereas Native Americans, who were hoped to eventually disappear through assimilation, needed to meet much higher blood quantum to be considered a real Indian and obtain any treaty rights. The roots of this system of white supremacy fueled the Indian reservation system, residential boarding schools, Jim Crow laws, separate but "equal," and even modern maladies such as the school-to-prisons pipeline and the use of excessive force on Black and brown bodies by law enforcement.

The modern settler-colonial cultural morality and spirituality are developed from a particular worldview. How we understand our world directly affects how we see the Scriptures. You've heard the saying, "garbage in, garbage out"? Well, a distorted worldview *in* equals a twisted theology and view of the Scriptures *out*. The inadequacy to understand the Scriptures from the more Indigenous perspective from which they were written, coupled with the hubris of white supremacy, has made many other approaches to hermeneutics or theology anathema, or at least relegated them to a subtext status, while elevating Western theology and interpretations to sacred status.

Questions for Reflecting

1. What are some of the things we can learn from creation?
2. Share some ways we might heighten our own conscience and then some ways that we might dull our own conscience. Can there be a group conscience? Explain your answer.
3. What are some ways community can serve to help us know God and become agents of change for good in the world?
4. How has the Western worldview been used to distort the way we understand the Holy Scriptures?

Chapter Seven

Human Spirituality without Religion

"Our Creator put us on this wide, rich land, and told us we were free to go where the game was, where the soil was good for planting. That was our state of true happiness."—Tenskwatawa, the Prophet (Shawnee), 1805

SIMPLY PUT, OUR MISSION is to align ourselves with God's mission, the *missio Dei*. Just as God sent Jesus to create, incarnate, and die for a world in which God could allow free moral beings to choose to live in loving harmony with God's self and all God created, we are being sent to serve those same purposes on earth. We are sent with a message of God's love for the whole community of creation that is embodied by the way in which we live our lives and that will cause others to want to hear our message. Our mission is to be inviting others into the community of Jesus, regardless of what it is called and regardless of whether or not they recognize him. We do this by ever extending the circle of joy and acceptance in our particular context.

I probably view religion like many Americans. When I think about religion, words come to mind like, *formal, strict, established, methodical, deep-seated*. These descriptive words are not critically negative statements about religion, but they characterize any spiritual system that has been around for awhile. Human beings are by nature spiritual, in that we seek meaning and higher purpose to our lives. Even the "new atheists" admit that human beings have developed internal ways (they might say "delusions") that people use to find happiness. Whether genetic or by other disposition, people are spiritual in that we all search for something beyond ourselves. When we organize the data from that search, we call it a religion. Here is my own succinct "textbook" definition of religion:

Human Spirituality without Religion

> A journey seeking that which is both outside ourselves (the quest for the Ultimate) and that which is inside ourselves (the quest for the Intimate) that results in the practice of our collective discoveries through our behavior, ritual, symbol, story, and ceremony.

Our spirituality may contain religion but the opposite may not be necessarily true. Any religion can become void of spirituality. Religions tend to be a strange mix of truth claims and pragmatism. Most religions are based upon a particular revelation in history, although often these religions have a somewhat obscure history (as in the case of all the world's major religions). The truth claims are important because the myth reflects the ways in which that particular religion works for the adherents. Religions answer deep need questions like, "Does the religion give people a sense of inner peace?" "Does it address social concerns?" "Does it give meaning to the mystery of higher purpose?" Everything beyond that people usually call "faith." If a religion's truth claims seem plausible and it seemingly *works* for people, all the better for that religion.

The problem is that most religions, as I have described them, are a modern phenomenon. Even the religions that predate modernity have by and large become modern. It is exactly for this reason that people are not responding to religion. Most of us, in whom our spirituality matters, want to be done with modernism and all its cold, mechanistic, production-oriented, dualistically driven forms. The current generation (and that includes people from all age groups) wants a spirituality that is not expressed in modernity's neat package. These folks seek another form of fulfillment to answer life's most ultimate and intimate questions. By and large, the trend is to seek out postmodern or pre-modern solutions. The religions that continue to emphasize pre-modern principles and values, like Buddhism and Hinduism, appear to be more stable. The draw of postmodernity has unfortunately been to continue down the scale of Enlightenment-bound modernity and into an advanced form of post-Enlightenment-bound secular materialism.

I am not trying to say that religion is going away. In fact, the most fundamentalist forms of religions, especially as this discussion pertains to Islam and Christianity, seem to be in resurgence. The presently popular fundamentalist response to postmodernity is to stop all the outside influences and silence all the new questions with old answers. It is also apparent today that fundamentalism's old answers to new questions are being spoken much louder and more harshly than they were in the past. Religion, it seems, is here to stay. The war of competing religious philosophies will no doubt continue as long as there are human beings, but that is not to say that religion does not change. Part and parcel of why people are rejecting modern religion is the pursuit to find for themselves ways of having more options. Any religion limiting basic forms of diversity is likely destined to wane in the near future.

On the positive side, globalization has created a new global awareness of "the cultural other." "The cultural other," in this context, can be defined as those people who seem to think, act, dress, eat, talk, and worship differently than us. Yet, as we all continue to learn about each other, it is difficult to maintain images of the cultural other as the two-dimensional depictions that might have only held up in our modern past. In fact, most of us have contact with the cultural other on a daily basis, and, most of us even enjoy those interactions. To one degree or another, we find the diversity of humanity not only necessary, but interesting.

A Native American Case Study

Religious diversity is not new to our continent. Over millennia, Native American tribes have formed a great many formal, strict, established, methodical, and deep-seated ways of expressing their faith. People sometimes refer to these diverse ways as tribal religions. By and large, these religions have been traditionally monotheistic, although some might view God as a creative force and a few tribes even have a system of lower deities serving the one Creator. Overwhelmingly, most Native American tribal religions are monotheistic and reference God in personal terms such as "Creator," "Great Spirit," or "Great Mystery." Although each tribe may have different creation stories, separate revelations of the sacred, various sacred objects and rituals, together they have much more in common than not. Remarkably unlike the experience in Europe, I know of no accounts of Indian wars fought over differing religious beliefs.

For good or bad, one thing that is always said about Native Americans is that they are a spiritual people. But what does that mean? Does it mean the white tribes are not spiritual? One thing it may mean for America's host people to be spiritual is what could be called "organic living," meaning traditional Native Americans tend to take life as it comes, giving each moment its due as it occurs. I also think Indigenous spirituality has something to do with earthiness. Maybe, insofar as this grounded spirituality is full of symbolism and ceremony (to the point where I have even heard folks call eagles, bears, and wolves "Indian animals"), it has to do with creation. More than that, I would say it tends to be more about how Indigenous people value creation and how we see our place in creation.

Native American spirituality is, in its essence, tied to the land. Indigenous people draw meaning as humans from a particular place. The place Indigenous people call home is always a geographic location and usually accompanied by covenant stories between the people and the Creator. The landmarks in that particular geographic location are not inanimate objects to Indigene but they hold special sacred significance. The rivers, the springs, the rain, the snow, the trees, the fields, and the mountains are all a source of life to Native Americans. These sacred places have a life that originates from the life force of creation.

The immediate reaction from some Enlightenment-bound minds when they hear creation spoken of in animate terms is to make accusations of "animism." Old habits die hard, and usually through education, so please allow me to address this issue further on in this book. For now, suffice it to assure you with certainty that Native Americans do not "worship nature." Like Western thinkers, Native Americans integrate a view of creation into a particular worldview and culture. But, unlike Western thinkers, Native Americans think about creation very differently than Western peoples. No one lives life in a cultural vacuum. Native American values are very ancient and even today are still very deeply rooted among America's First Nations. Like most peoples, Native Americans feel that happiness and well-being are goals to be sought after in this life and in the afterlife.

It is true that traditional Indigenous values are in decline as a result of a number of factors, including modernity, the premature death of elders and spiritual leaders, forced cultural assimilation, and surviving a near genocide. In order for our Native American people to find a restored sense of well-being we may need to act more decisively about recovering those declining values that produce a sense of well-being. The fact that our values are waning makes it even more critical for non-natives to begin the learning process at once. This is a critical time in America's history. We may now be entering the last chance for the dominant culture to learn the lessons intended by God over five hundred years ago, from Native Americans. The window of opportunity is closing as surely as the impending disaster that awaits us if they are not recovered.

One of the great pan-Indian movements in this country occurred at the turn of the eighteenth to the nineteenth century. Tecumseh and his brother "the Prophet" were Shawnee Indian leaders who tried to unite all the Indian nations in order to hold off the advancement of the white Americans to a place east of the Allegheny and Appalachian Mountains. Indeed, American history and culture might have taken a very different route if these insightful leaders had been able to form a more successful alliance with the eastern and southern tribes before November, 1811, when the newly formed Indian alliance capital of Prophetstown was decimated. Tecumseh's brother, also known as Tenskwatawa, supplied much of the spiritual vision for the movement.

As evidenced by his speech, Tenskwatawa was searching for something two hundred years ago that was similar to what we are all trying to find today. He was trying to find a way for the host people of America to recover their naturally endowed values while confronting acculturation in the form of Euro-American encroachment and modernity. The same problem identified by Tenskwatawa in his day not only applies to present-day Indigenous communities but to modern America as a whole. These words of the Shawnee leader Tenskwatawa were recorded in 1805, at the height of the movement.

> Our Creator put us on this wide, rich land, and told us we were free to go where the game was, where the soil was good for planting. That was our state of true happiness. We did not have to beg for anything. Our Creator had taught us how to find and make everything we needed, from trees and plants and animals and stone. We lived in bark, and we wore only the skins of animals. Our Creator taught us how to use fire, in living, and in sacred ceremonies. He taught us how to heal with barks and roots, and how to make sweet foods with berries and fruits, with papaws and the water of the maple tree. Our Creator gave us tobacco, and said, "Send your prayers up to me on its fragrant smoke." Our Creator taught us how to enjoy loving our mates, and gave us laws to live by, so that we would not bother each other, but help each other. Our Creator sang to us in the wind and the running water, in the bird songs, in children's laughter, and taught us music. And we listened, and our stomachs were never dirty and never troubled us.
>
> Thus, were we created. Thus, we lived for a long time, proud and happy. We had never eaten pig meat, nor tasted the poison called whiskey, nor worn wool from sheep, nor struck fire or dug earth with steel, nor cooked in iron, nor hunted and fought with loud guns, nor ever had diseases which soured our blood or rotted our organs. We were pure, so we were strong and happy.

But, beyond the Great Sunrise Water, there lived a people who had iron, and those dirty and unnatural things, who seethed with diseases, who fought to death over the names of their gods! They had so crowded and befouled their own island that they fled from it, because excrement and carrion were up to their knees. They came to our island. Our Singers had warned us that a pale people would come across the Great Water and try to destroy us, but we forgot. We did not know they were evil, so we welcomed them and fed them. We taught them much of what Our Grandmother had taught us, how to hunt, grow corn and tobacco, and find good things in the forest. They saw how much room we had, and wanted it. They brought iron and pigs and wool and rum and disease. They came farther and drove us over the mountains. Then when they had filled up and dirtied our old lands by the sea, they looked over the mountains and saw this Middle Ground, and we are old enough to remember when they started rushing into it. We remember our villages on fire every year and the crops slashed every fall and the children hungry every winter. All this you know.

For many years we traded furs to the English or the French, for wool blankets and guns and iron things, for steel awls and needles and axes, for mirrors, for pretty things made of beads and silver, and for liquor. This was foolish, but we did not know it. We shut our ears to the Great Good Spirit. We did not want to hear that we were being foolish.

But now those things of the white men have corrupted us, and made us weak and needful. Our men forgot how to hunt without noisy guns. Our women don't want to make fire without steel, or cook without iron, or sew without metal awls and needles, or fish without steel hooks. Some look in those mirrors all the time, and no longer teach their daughters to make leather or render bear oil. We learned to need the white men's goods, and so now a People who never had to beg for anything must beg for everything!

Some of our women married white men, and made halfbreeds. Many of us now crave liquor. He whose filthy name I will not speak, he who was I before, was one of the worst of those drunkards. There are drunkards in almost every family. You know how bad this is.

And so, you see what has happened to us. We were fools to take all these things that weakened us. We did not need them then, but we believe we need them now. We turned our backs on the old ways. Instead of thanking Weshemoneto for all we used to have, we turned to the white men and asked them for more. So now we depend upon the very people who destroy us! This is our weakness! Our corruption! Our Creator scolded me, "If you had lived the way I taught you, the white men could never have got you under their foot!"[1]

At first glance, a reader from the dominant American culture may be tempted to view Tenskwatawa's observations as simplistic and ethnocentric. They are not. He is not simply saying, "Indian always equals good, white always equals bad." Tenskwatawa rather talks from his personal experiences and observations. He specifically shares what was very good about Native American life and what he sees that is wrong with white society, insofar as how they have affected Native Americans. Furthermore, Tenskwatawa is critical of the current situation among Native Americans in his own time. And please do remember as you juxtapose the concurrent events, this speech took place around the same time the "heathen school" was becoming a reality just a few states over.

If Tenskwatawa's speech sounds bigoted to you, please remember that he was speaking at a time when his tribe and family were literally being killed and driven from their land just because they were Indian. The Shawnee people were facing true systemic racism and ethnocide. Even given his desperate circumstances, I still understand Tenskwatawa's observations are as poignant today for our current dilemma as they were over two centuries ago. Here are a few general observations.

First of all, Tenskwatawa noted that prior to European contact, Indian people were given their land by the Creator. Is that something you have ever considered? In Acts 17:26 it states, "From one man he created all the nations throughout the whole earth. He decided beforehand when they should rise and fall, and he determined their boundaries." If it is God who determines each nation's borders, we should ask how God feels about those who move those borders illegally. In fact, several references in the Older Testament forbid and condemn those who move their neighbor's property markers.

The issue at hand is not to go further here about land theft (I'll leave that for another day), but to show the deep significance of the homelands of each Native American nation. Since both Native American belief and the Christian Scriptures bear out that the land is a gift from God, it makes good sense that Native American spirituality is literally grounded in each particular tribal group's gifted land. Any gift from God is sacred. How much more is the very ground sacred when it is given in covenant by Creator?

---

1. In Miller, "Prophet and Tecumseh."

Secondly, Tenskwatawa acknowledged that Native Americans were happy and that they were self-sustaining, free, and spiritual people. Happiness really is important to any people group. Just so we don't get bogged down on terms, try to think of happiness not as the kind of selfish happiness going around today. I want to you think about the kind of happiness being described as *well-being*. Well-being takes account of our health, our ability to make a living, our hope toward a good future, and it also includes our own feelings of happiness. I think this is what the Prophet meant when he said Native Americans were "happy."

Well-being doesn't need to mean that things are perfect. In fact, no one is saying the life of Native American peoples was perfect before 1491. But precontact among many tribes (white contact occurred from 1491 through the mid-1800s) is remembered in terms of fondness as being happy times. I have had the good fortune of spending time with elders who were born shortly after the first white contact with their own tribal group, still living in the kind of era we are discussing. They always referred to those times as harder, but happier.

Thirdly, Tenskwatawa had something valuable to share but he did not see it extending beyond his own Native American people. Perhaps he could not see it because he viewed white people as being "diseased," "dirty," in religious turmoil, evil, covetous, and polluters. Again, this might sound bigoted, but allow me to explain what he was saying.

In the eighteenth century, European standards of bathing were far different than today. Bathing during this time period was considered to be a cause of disease and it was avoided as much as possible by the Europeans immigrants. On the contrary, most Native Americans had the habit of bathing daily. Tenskwatawa's observations were correct, even though there is likely some disdain coming from him concerning the cultural differences.

As for Tenskwatawa's comments concerning disease, we must remember that Native Americans had little disease prior to the arrival of the Europeans. All epidemics in America were introduced to by the Europeans. It was wholly factual for Tenskwatawa to condemn the Europeans as diseased, although for the most part (with notable exceptions) it was not their intention to spread disease.

According to some calculations, 90 to 95 percent of Native Americans may have died soon after contact with the European immigrants from the microbes brought by them. The theory is that microbes of smallpox, influenza, whooping cough, and so forth were hosted by the European animals, especially swine. As these animals reproduced and became feral, the disease microbes transferred themselves into the deer, turkey, and other game that were food staples for most Native Americans.[2] As one writer put it,

> The "savages" most of the colonists saw, without ever realizing it, were usually the traumatized, destitute survivors of ancient and intricate civilizations that had collapsed almost overnight. Even the superabundant "nature" the Europeans inherited had been largely put in place by these now absent gardeners, and had run wild only after they had ceased to cull and harvest it.[3]

In other words, the disease spread faster than the colonists. The devastation that occurred among various Native American tribes often took its toll prior to them ever seeing a white man. By the start of the nineteenth century, Tenskwatawa understood all too well who introduced the diseases to his people.

Concerning Tenskwatawa's remarks about religious turmoil among the white tribes, remember there were denominational splits occurring and even religious wars in Europe at the time. And concerning covetousness, one would be hard-pressed to make an argument that the Euro-Americans were not coveting their Native neighbor's lands, given the fact that whole tribes were being forced to relocate so non-Indians could have their property.

All in all, what Tenskwatawa said may seem harsh to us today but it was strikingly true to Tenskwatawa at the time. He had no romantic visions of a utopian time but he had the keen insight to understand what the future held for America. Similar testimony by other past and present Native American leaders can be easily found, but perhaps none give as much detail as Tenskwatawa. Tenskwatawa's view is clear. Native peoples were beginning to lose something that once held them together. The sad fact is that this loss continues today, but, ironically, it is the very remedy that is needed in our modern American society.

For that reason and others, we must not delay in considering what spiritual understandings were present for thousands of years among the host peoples of America. We should try to find out exactly what the lessons may have been that God was trying to teach the new Euro-immigrants. I am convinced that the less we know of these deep values, the poorer we

---

2. See Mann, *1491*.
3. Baker, "1491."

all are. We must address our deficit until we reclaim and restore America's waning Aboriginal values.

Fourthly, there are several other reasons why I chose to focus on Tenskwatawa's dilemma in this book. He and his brother Tecumseh were leaders in an inter-tribal movement that, if successful, might have changed the terms of how power was negotiated in the early Western frontier. In a sense, the defeat of Tecumseh and the failure to understand Native American values during that time in our history can be viewed as a microcosm of our situation over two hundred years later.

As it turned out, Indian fighter (and later president) William Henry Harrison defeated Tecumseh and the allied Indian tribes. The Indians were bitterly subjugated and the white tribes took over the frontier. From that point forward the white tribes could not be stopped, but only hindered by a few small resistance movements here and there (Geronimo, Little Big Horn, and others). The white tribes prospered and took over the whole nation. The reservation era followed and then the boarding school era ensued, and Indians began the recurrent mourning over the loss of their lives, land, families, religion, and traditions. In some ways the magnitude of grief suffered and the generational accumulation of traumatic stress made Native Americans susceptible to even more diseases, such as alcoholism, suicide epidemics, and so forth. But for the most part, by some miraculous phenomenon, America's host people still survive today.

Fifthly, another reason that I wanted to share about Tenskwatawa is that he was a survivor. Tenskwatawa personally recovered from being a victim of colonialism's vices. In Tenskwatawa's early years he became addicted to alcohol. Like so many Indian people in our time, he had to "hit bottom" in order to see a way back up to the good way that Creator intended for him to live. Experiencing his near destruction from the vices that accompanied the colonial oppression gave him a unique vantage point.

As with anyone who continues to experience a full recovery state, Tenskwatawa's perspective is not so much as a victim, but rather as one who has been empowered to lead others because of his former, unfortunate circumstances. I believe that there are many Native Americans now who have gone through similar trials and they are now ready to lead. I feel that one of the many ways they could be asked to lead in this country and in the church is by sharing their deep spiritual values.

We can gain some understanding of how far those Native Americans in Tenskwatawa's time had drifted by observing how high a standard of happiness he viewed as being in common. Tenskwatawa does not hesitate to place the blame upon his own people for allowing these negative values and practices to creep into the everyday life of the Indian. He calls his own people "foolish" and "weak," while reporting the bad news that the Creator also holds them to be responsible. Through Tenskwatawa's eyes we are able to get an idea of how disruptive the negative values of white supremacy really were upon Indian societies, during what was a crucial time of modernity's influence on large numbers of Native Americans.

Finally, Tenskwatawa set forth a spiritual vision. He envisioned the path that they (and we) must find again in order to be whole. It was a spiritual path, not necessarily a religious path. That path, I will argue, is deeply rooted in Native North American values, which have always been considerably different than many of the values of the dominant Euro-Americans. That path of well-being is deeply spiritual. It is what I refer to in this book as the "Harmony Way." As I said earlier, the Harmony Way is to Native Americans what shalom in Scripture was to the Jews (including Jesus). Because the revelation of the Harmony Way, shalom is unique to America's Indigenous peoples. It therefore must be understood as an American Harmony Way. It is a truly unique form of American shalom that we can call the Harmony Way.

An American Shalom

The Harmony Way is a way of living that undergirds all of Native American history, religion, traditions, ceremonies, story, social interaction, philosophy, and so forth, and it is found within a particular worldview that encompasses both being and doing in life, according to a set of values that are interconnected and that construct a meaningful whole. Jerry Gill's insights are helpful. He understands harmony and balance as two related concepts, but I have found no significant distinguishing characteristics in my own research and understanding. Nonetheless, Gill has much of importance to say.

> The two basic concepts that underlie nearly every Native American worldview are harmony and balance. It is the responsibility of the entire community to see to it that a proper harmony is maintained among the various aspects of the complex processes by which the world is woven together . . . The order and dynamic of reality are continuously renewed through harmonious participation in these

patterns and processes. The success of an individual results from the quality of his or her desire and ability a proper balance on the path of life. . . . The main resources available in this endeavor, in addition to parental guidance and example, are traditional beliefs and teachings. When a person fails to achieve or maintain this desired balance, straying or falling from the prescribed path, he or she is said to have become "sick."[4]

Understanding the lack of maintaining harmony as a sickness seems to parallel both Tenskwatawa's concerns and my own. Like Tenskwatawa, I am looking to our inherent American values for a Native American concept, or a way of living and being in harmony and balance. Such a concept can help all American people make sense of the ubiquitous culture of colonization in which all Americans, especially Native Americans, now reside. My research has led me to believe that at least part of the answer to the lies of colonial empire are to be found in the rediscovery of the Native American Harmony Way, because it contains so many of both Native American and the Jesus Way's core values.

If we are to follow Jesus, which is to be healed/saved and bring about healing/salvation in the world, therefore, our healing/salvation, along with the healing/salvation of the rest of the community of creation, is the essence of the gospel itself, and what we do as co-laborers with God is how we work out that healing/salvation. Faith formulas and religious devotion are all well and good, and confession of faith is an act of identity, but God knows our heart. Songs and chants of devotion are a witness to ourselves and others but Creator does not need them. All the old "proofs" of faith, including the creeds of the church, can be helpful in various ways, as long as they are not used to exclude others, but they are not the prime-product that demonstrates our healing and attests to our faith. Instead, they are the by-product of our revealed faith as we partake in God's healing of the world.

Questions for Reflecting

1. What are some of the distinctions that we can draw between religion and spirituality?

2. Who is the cultural other to you? With whom are you the cultural other? Be specific.

4. Gill, *Native American Worldviews*, 141–42.

3. What of the lessons from Tenskwatawa's speech can be applied to us today? In what ways?
4. Have you ever made a connection between salvation and shalom? What might be some of the connecting points?

Chapter Eight

Reframing Old Constructs

"The world as we have created it is a process of our thinking. It cannot be changed without changing our thinking."—ALBERT EINSTEIN

MANY RELIGIONS SUCH AS Christianity, Buddhism, and Hinduism, and evolution alike, espouse ideas that purport or imply that human beings are at the pinnacle of the created order, be it as created, reincarnated, or part of an evolutionary order. On the other hand, Indigenous creation narratives invariably reveal human beings as simply a part of the rest of creation, participating with creation in an important role, usually as caretakers. Those creation narratives without human beings' isolated singularity aid in reminding us that creation *can* exist without us. The gift of our healing comes as a result of our participation with Creator in bringing healing on the earth. We are, as the story in Genesis 2:6-7 goes, creatures of earth. "And the LORD God formed a man's body from the dust of the ground and breathed into it the breath of life. And the man became a living person." The Scripture suggests that human beings are finely crafted with two elements, earth and spirit, sacred earth and sacred breath—not as two separated elements but as one integrated being. In reality, human beings are made of one essence expressed by two symbiotic materials:

- <u>Earth</u> (organic elements, minerals, water, salts, and trace elements) and,
- <u>Spirit</u> (the breath of Great Spirit—all that is beyond the physical)

We dare not divide ourselves as bipartite or tripartite persons, or even seriously consider choosing a salvation for our soul without it being inexplicably linked to our bodies. Healing or salvation requires the full measure of both as one. Even the word *humus,* from which we derive *human,* is connected to the organic soil, animated by billions of living organisms.

Salvation/healing is not a matter simply of the ethereal realm but must include the material to be complete. We dare not seriously consider a heaven that has more importance to us later than this time on earth does now, lest we become what so many in the faith community have become: namely, so heavenly minded we are no earthly good. When speaking of traditional Cherokee religion, Keetoowah Cherokee spiritual leader Redbird Smith said, "This religion does not teach me to concern myself of the life that shall be after this, but it does teach me to be concerned with what my everyday life should be."[1] Smith's understanding reminds me of Jesus' message in Matthew 6:34: "So don't worry about tomorrow, for tomorrow will bring its own worries. Today's trouble is enough for today."

The biblical concept of salvation is broad, and in many ways can be equated directly with the Native American concept of restoration or harmony. The Creator's plan for harmony concerns all of creation, not just humanity. In fact, human beings appear to be the only creatures on earth who willfully reject their created state and therefore must make the choice to return to normalcy, which is a state of harmony. That includes repairing the damage they have caused in human relationships and with the whole community of creation. This restoration to normalcy, to the Harmony Way, can occur through many truth paths, but if you are a Christian you will likely believe that, ultimately, each path leads to Christ and has implications for all of creation and our earthly context.

If we are to take context seriously among Indigenous peoples or anyone else then it requires reframing former European-based approaches. Western Christianity's problem with Platonic dualism and the worldview it produced, including epistemologies, theologies, and missiologies, developed from that limited worldview. The old constructs held within these frameworks must be abandoned in favor of more contextual approaches. Otherwise, Indigenous and other Christian faiths will merely reflect to hollow forms of colonial Westernization.

---

1. Quoted in Young, *Quest for Harmony,* 149.

Reframing Old Constructs
Salvation and Healing

The religiously oriented word for one's relationship to God is, at least in Christianity, *salvation*. Whether people are "saved from" something or "saved for" something, the other side of being lost is to be saved. The emphasis on one's lostness seems to be primary in Western forms of Christianity. Could it be that the binary thinking, so ever present in the Western worldview, has driven the theology of lostness versus salvation as an absolute binary? Such binary thinking has especially been justified by the doctrine of original sin. If people are totally lost, and their "nature" has been corrupted by "human sinfulness," then salvation is their only chance at redemption. Indeed, salvation becomes their only virtue. Such teaching is especially convenient when the church is merged with the state and the educated elite become the primary interpreters of Scripture.

The salvation construct has taken on added characteristics, especially in evangelical Christianity, as it connotes a particular code of beliefs, such as the virgin birth, one's strict, mostly literal view of Scripture, and the imminent physical return of Jesus to earth. Subscription to the evangelical doctrinal prescription reduces what was apparently meant to be a whole lifestyle down to assent to a particular set of beliefs. I would argue the word *salvation* is not only out of step with the cultural context in which we live, but that it is so laden with cultural baggage that it has lost its original intention. To be "saved" in Christianity has come to mean one is saved from the world and saved to a particular static, doctrinally loaded, religious bubble. In other words, salvation has come to mean a separation from the world in which we live.

I am quite sure that how the word is currently used in American culture has little to do with its scriptural use. When we examine Scriptures like, "Now is our salvation much closer than when we first began" (Rom 13:11), we are forced to expand today's understanding to a broader sense of the word. The concept of healing or healings includes our emotions, our mind, our spirit, our soul, our bodies, our relationships to the whole community of creation—and it can be continuous, not static. The broader sense of the salvation construct is perhaps better manifest in the word *healing*.

Healing comes in many forms and can be expressed in a variety of ways. In the case of Scripture passages like, "Now is our healing is much closer than when we first began," Paul is saying we were at some time in the past healed in our initial acceptance of God's love through Jesus; we are continuing to be healed as we mature in God's love and understand the vast applications of that love in the world, and we will be healed in some form in the future upon the finality of our lives by death. Healing, certainly a major component of traditional interpretations of the word *salvation*, has even broader connotations than the modern view of salvation. Healing encompasses an ongoing relationship with God without making it irrelevant to the rest of the world. Not only does everyone need healing, everyone wants to be healed. Healing is universal and can apply to anyone.

Try substituting the word *healing* for *salvation* anywhere in the Second Testament and in most cases, it actually makes more sense, without narrowing the concept or bifurcating it. Take for example Luke 19:9, the story of Zacchaeus, a place where the most narrow modern view of salvation does not fit well. "Jesus responded, 'Salvation has come to this home today, for this man has shown himself to be a true son of Abraham.'" Here is a greedy man who wins eternal salvation simply by paying his debts and providing reparations for his extortion. The Scripture, taken literally under the modern construct of salvation, would mean there is an alternative way, aside from the presumed, modern, prescriptive way of correct beliefs, to find salvation. When giving preference to the wider, healing aspects of salvation, the Scripture makes more sense and is far more relatable.

Kingdom and Community

One concept in the Scriptures that might be helpful to explore in mission is that of "kingdom." The idea of a "new kingdom," as Jesus spoke of it, is about finding a whole new way of doing things—a new paradigm, if you will. In our day, the idea of the biblical "kingdom" is a difficult one to convey. Howard Snyder states,

> The Bible is full of God's kingdom. This is most clear, of course, in passages, which speak directly of God's kingly rule. But kingdom surprises appear if we look at Scripture through a broader lens. We learn more about the kingdom when we view all of Scripture as the history of God's "economy" or plan to restore a fallen creation, bringing all God has made—woman, man and their total environment—to the fulfillment of his purposes under his sovereign reign.[2]

---

2. Snyder, *Kingdom, Church, and World*, 17.

Reframing Old Constructs

I agree with Snyder that the concept is surprisingly ubiquitous throughout the Scriptures and that *kingdom* is an overarching theme, encompassing all of life. I would go further just to state that the kingdom Jesus spoke of, including its intended king, is *the* primary overarching theme of the Scriptures. This theme is often voiced in the Older Testament as shalom and Jubilee, whereas Jesus speaks directly of a kingdom.

The term *kingdom* is not perfectly suited for us since most of us live our lives without allegiance to a particular earthly king. In the past, kingdom has always had a military association, but as yet I have not found other words that can convey the radical intent. My injunction is for the reader to read "kingdom of harmony" when they see the word *kingdom*. The kingdom is the intended way of living and being desired by the Creator. In this sense it is closely connected with harmony and the core values associated with the Native American Harmony Way or shalom.

Jesus originally spoke in Middle Eastern metaphors, not Western European translations of them. I don't see a right or wrong answer here, only a choice of metaphors. The imperial Church has, in and of itself, perpetuated a "kingdom" quite apart from the love and work of Christ, and is often referred to as Christendom. With Christ's name used so closely in conjunction with the evil system mentioned, I wonder if it is not time to rethink our metaphors in order not to confuse Christ with the evils of Christendom or even with the evils perpetrated by Christianity. If I were to seriously consider a one-to-one literal metaphor of the word kingdom for our day, perhaps it would better be translated "the Global Corporation of God," having God as our "CEO." But that does not really work for me either, and I prefer the community of creation.

So, shall we try it out? "The community of creation is within you." I very much understand this better in my own experience. It speaks to me of my connection to all other creation. The theme of God's "rule and reign" is definitely a theme across the whole of Scripture. The theme is about a shalom reign. *Community of Creator* is the term I use for Trinity. If you are Trinitarian (and I am), community of creation is another link to Trinity. In this metaphor, the community of Creator invites us to become (what already is and will eventually fully be) the community of creation.

Mission and the Cultural Other

Holiness and Wholeness

Purity culture in religion often has the opposite outcome to what is expected. Whether it be a pledge to celibacy in the priesthood, or harsh rules of not wearing your hair a particular way, women not speaking in church or teaching, not wearing makeup, not dancing, wearing an additional article of clothing, or any other outward manifestation worn as a badge of humility, sanctity, or holiness, these things often produce the same result: impurity. The human drive towards perfection is both crippling and unnecessary. We need not be flawless before God; we need only be human.

When our efforts move toward trying to be perfect, we become in danger of practicing idolatry. Becoming like God isn't about a measure of perfection. When Jesus says in Matthew 5:48, "be perfect even as your father in heaven is perfect," to strive for some sort of moral proximity to Creator is a misunderstanding of what has been stated. For human beings to be perfect is to fulfill the role we have been given. God fulfills God's role perfectly and continues to do it daily; that fulfillment of "goodness" is being the perfect God. Our role is to be human. To be human means we are inherently limited. To accept our limitedness, to accept our humanity, means we are dependent on God, and on others in the whole community of creation.

The real question is not, "Can we be perfect in a comparison of ourselves to God?" That question almost always produces poor results, frustration, and anxiety. The more appropriate question is, "What has Creator made us to be?" My understanding is that being human is foundational to being harmony makers and restorers of balance on earth, among the rest of the community of creation. This human role of creating, maintaining, and repairing harmony when it is broken has nothing to do with perfection as it is meant in the Greek understanding. That type of perfection has more to do with flawlessness than it does fulfillment of purpose. When I attempt flawlessness, I am just setting myself up for failure, which leads to guilt, shame, and self-degradation on one hand, and on the other rationalization, the invention of theologies that excuse me or an unhealthy view of my own power in some godlike complex, affording me the right to us my power over others.

To spend our lives trying to be flawless is one long exercise in futility and vanity. Instead, we should seek to fulfill our human role, and when we do that, when we act like limited humans, fulfilling our particular purpose, we are being perfect. Like God, we are fulfilling our role in the community of creation. Accepting our role and our limitedness is actually what makes us most spiritual. There's a line in the movie *Rudy* where the priest tells Rudy, "There are two things I know for certain: One, there is a God, and two, I'm not him." This says it pretty plainly. I have no need to control God and God has no need to control me. We perfectly fulfill our own purposes together. God as God, myself as human.

Our role as human beings is one we must exercise in the context of the whole community of creation. If we merely understand our role in an individualistic context, we miss viewing the whole. Human beings were made to live in cooperative community. Our wholeness is only achieved when we find our place in both the human community and by taking responsibility to maintain harmony with the rest of the whole community of creation, including the four-legged ones, the crawling ones, the flying ones, those that swim, the plant world, and even the micro-organisms all around (and in) us. God intends for the whole earth to be healed, not just humans and not just human "souls." Personal salvation is an overrated system, focusing on what the individual receives rather than what God intends for healing a person in the context of a much larger community. When our theologies lean more toward a person's "soul" being saved rather than a whole community being healed, including human and nonhuman actors, and even the earth herself, we have surely missed the mark. An individual's healing is a by-product of God's love, not the prime product. Disembodied theologies—mental assent without embodied belief and action in one's whole community—miss the mark and play into Platonic dualism, giving more weight to the ethereal than the material. We are both/and, and so much more than either alone.

Church and Gathering

To go to church is not to be the church. The ecclesia are those called who embody Christ's purpose on earth. The context is one's community and the world and we can tell by Jesus' context. Jesus leaves the Trinity, the community of Creator, for the purpose of healing the earth that he made. His tools are only those of his own DNA in the Godhead, which includes deference to the other's well-being, celebration of diversity, truth, vulnerability, humility, respect, and joy. Jesus exhibits these same values and others, leaving a group of followers to spread this good news of healing for the whole world. Healing for the whole world is not expressed through domination of other human beings or by dominating the earth and the earth's creatures. Healing for the world is accomplished by creating models that others can see and those of which they can become a part. A church that practices shalom is a healing church for the whole community of creation, and particularly in tangible ways in their local community.

In Luke 15 Jesus shares three stories that are actually just one story. The parables of the Lost Sheep, the Lost Coin, and the Lost Son are really just one parable of the Lost Elder Brother. The context is Luke 15:1–2: "Tax collectors and other notorious sinners often came to listen to Jesus teach. This made the Pharisees and teachers of religious law complain that he was associating with such sinful people—even eating with them!" Before we are too tough on these particular Pharisees, let's remember the Pharisees' duties included feeding the poor. The specific difference in this story was that Jesus was eating with them, granting them his peace and expressing equality with the so-called "lost."

People do lose their way in life. In these stories Jesus conceded to the Pharisees that there are lost people. The lost sheep, coin, and son are metaphors that allow the Pharisees their initial judgment, but these particular metaphors are not neutral whatsoever. Jesus calls the Pharisees to think of themselves as shepherds. Doing so, he to asks them to lower themselves to the status of a disparaged profession, usually held by Gentiles. Then he asks them to think of themselves as a woman, most likely a widow, which was equally insulting to the Pharisees. Jesus' wisdom forces them, after the two prior stories, to choose the lesser of the three evils in their minds, the loving father. Even though the lost son did not deserve acceptance in their minds, the Pharisees might find in this waiting father some semblance of identification.

The Pharisees Jesus was addressing would have found the lost son's sins inexcusable and they must have balked when Jesus portrayed this loving father as one not interested in the son's speech relegating himself to the status of a hired servant. Especially of note is the father's position as one who was watching and waiting, hoping for the son's return. "And while he was a long way off" the father ran to him, gifting him with precious items and announcing his return to the whole community and calling for festivities to celebrate! Jesus was pulling them in the story. Jesus was asking them if they could somehow find the joy of celebration in sitting down and eating with those they considered lost.

After the story seems complete, the punch line, so to speak, had not yet been told. Ah, there was a minor character in the story missing, namely the elder brother. In the case of each parable there is both joy over every lost entity, and the whole community called to celebrate that joy. Each sub-story has its own party-packed ending but the final ending of the whole parable is of the father and the elder son talking about the elder son coming to join the festivities. The story concludes with the elder son outside the party, but also, the story is a demonstration of the father's love for both sons. The Pharisees understood well that Jesus was calling them back to experience God's love for them, by taking a seat with Jesus at the table of the lost. The point of their neglect of their own standards was made clear through the particular holy triad of Israel's shalom ethic, which involved taking care of the foreign immigrant, the widows, and the orphans. By Jesus' use of a foreign shepherd, a widow who lost one of her coins, and two sons who actually made themselves orphans, everyone understood the point of the parable.

Communities are made up of people who are in one way or another lost. To be lost is not a lack of subscription to a particular set of beliefs or doctrines. To some degree, because we all are human, we all need each other's help to fulfill our purpose on earth. To be lost is to be out of communion with the community, to be isolated and alone, whether in proximity or alone in our own souls. We are all shades of lost regardless of our beliefs. Belonging, though, should always proceed belief, and belief should never be the litmus test for belonging. What we do, in actuality, is what we actually believe.

Bible and Scriptures

As an evangelical I was taught to believe that regardless of apparent contradictions and inconsistencies, every word in the Bible was true. This included words like those of God's instructions to Joshua to commit genocide on the Canaanites, including every man, woman, and child, and all their animals as well. Beyond this total and complete view of the words of the Bible, I was told to believe that God's sure hand guided not just the authors, but the transcribers and the councils who approved the writings, to create a perfect book, out of sixty-six documents written over a 1,300-year period by Jews and Christians. Ironically, most Jewish traditions do not hold the same level of foundationalism as do most Christian traditions. Not only is there space for discussion (midrash) in Judaism, but it is considered a necessity to consider various interpretations. The problem, of course, with the explanation of the Bible in the most literal terms is that, number one, the people who constructed those documents never meant for them to be interpreted that way, and number two, the belief in what I call the "magic book theory" takes more faith than it does to believe its content. This rises to a level of devotion to, or worship of, the Bible with the Bible on the same level as deity.

The writers of most of Scripture, especially the Second Testament, had no conception of a Bible, in the sense that we know it today. Nor do I think they wanted their words chaptered, numbered, sliced and diced, and interpreted from a Western worldview. Neither Paul nor anyone else in his day could have imagined writing a letter to solve a particular problem among a group of Jesus followers, expecting those words to be examined individually, seeking out the deepest meaning for each word and applying each word to a broad Western-based theology. In the Western worldview, extrinsic categories are created that take away from the whole, draining one's thoughts of the original intentions and creating new, and often irrelevant, subcategories. No one in the Scriptures spoke from an Enlightenment-bound, Western worldview.

Most of Scripture is story. There is a world of difference in how modern Western people interpret story and how non-Western people do. Indigenous and many non-Western understandings of story do not generally ask about the meaning of each word, nor do they assume the story is literal, but rather they seek to understand the truth of the story for themselves or their group. Neither do they universalize every truth they discover.

Often the beauty of a whole story gets lost in the Western anxiety to fit every part of it into a Western theological narrative. For example, the first few chapters of Genesis, which I think we might all agree are important, is about a harmonious and balanced earth, created by a God of harmony and beauty, being disrupted by people's mistakes. Those stories strike me as Creator's good intentions for the whole world and the way humanity must realize our limitedness, and with God's help, hope that we can restore the balance in the world among the whole community of creation.

Western theology has created from this section of Scripture a theology of a literal seven-day creation, a universal doctrine of original sin, and the inability of humans to restore harmony in the world except through a particular formula of belief. In the West, disagreements over these doctrines have been used for the cause of war, burning people at the stake, and other methods for the disposal of heretics, such as drowning or being crushed to death with rocks. Denominational splits, sometimes rippling to many other splits, have occurred repeatedly and the base of power from which the church has drawn has been declared by some to be the only power capable of granting salvation.

There is something deeply wrong about construing the Bible so that it would cause people to elevate their power over others to the point of harm, when the founder of the religion said they are to love their enemies. Taking the argument as a whole, remember that Christians are here expected not only have faith in the book, but also in the many councils, interpreters, theologians, kings, and popes throughout the history of its making and interpretation. The Bible is full of contradictions and dissimilarities, and that's okay as long as one does not subscribe to the "magic book" theory. The stories are worthy of serious consideration, but some are simply story, and not to be taken literally or torn into parts.

Some portions of Scripture are poetry and wisdom, some are historical records. Most of the books in the Second Testament are corrective letters and should not be taken out of that particular context. Only the four Gospels were ever meant to be universalized in the same way Christians universalize the whole Bible, and even then, there are different styles of writing within the four Gospels, to be understood differently. As with any 2,000-plus-year-old document, of which none of the originals have ever been found, those Scriptures should be examined carefully, not used casually, and, before they are used to harm another member of the community of creation, taken with a grain of salt. On the positive side, epic stories, such as those in Scripture, have a surplus of meaning, and teach many truths, not just those narrowly taught in evangelicalism.

Summary

Much of Western faith is not based upon reality. Because Native American and other Indigenous spiritualities are so much a part of everyday reality it is sometimes difficult to parse or categorize it. Even when one searches the indexes of books written by Indigenous scholars, spirituality is very seldom listed as if it were a separate subject. While thinking about spirituality in Western terms we sometimes refer to Indigenous spirituality as religion, but religion is usually thought of in the terms I expressed earlier or in one of two binary tracks, something either internally private or externally public. In the Indian way of understanding religion there is no difference between private, public, or other spheres of thought or expression. Spirituality is inseparable from Indigenous life and thought. It is woven into the very fabric of being Indigenous. Native American spirituality in this aspect of understanding is similar to other Indigenous people in the world. In speaking of Melanesian worldview concerning religion, Henry Paroi comments,

> Defining an area called religion is a typical Western approach to life, for it requires separating one aspect of life from others.... For Melanesians, it seems more accurate not to separate religion from politics or economics or kinship. That is, religion is not limited to the sacred and supernatural, but it is a way of integrating and managing life.... There is no distinction between the sacred and the profane in typical Melanesian thinking because the total world is put together by religion.[3]

Spirituality among Indigenous peoples is a natural constituent of everything, while even the idea of a spiritual worldview can be viewed as ethereal in a more dualistic worldview. To Indigenous people spirituality is very tangible. For Native Americans, whether it is ceremony or just the way we conduct ourselves on a daily basis, the entirety of life is considered to be a sacred, spiritual path and any accompanying ritual is a symbol of that path.

For example, many traditional Cherokee Indians begin each morning with prayer and a type of self-baptism at a river or creek. Some traditional Washoe Indians begin the day by washing their face with water, preferably with water from Lake Tahoe. Muskogee tribal people often face the morning sun for their daily prayers and many traditional Kiowa Indians burn cedar each morning. Each tribe has its own version of morning prayers.[4] These morning prayer-times remind our people that each day and everything in the day is sacred. Native American spirituality is expressed tangibly using water, sunlight, smoke, and many other symbols, but it is also wholly integrated in our hearts.

The core values of most North American Indigenous communities are drastically different than those of the dominant society. Consider one Native American man's experience of which many Indians can resonate.

> Whenever I travel back to Oklahoma... I struggle with my [later] return to the city. As soon as I get back to New York, I feel as

---

3. Rynkiewich, ed., *Land and Churches in Melanesia*, 169–70.

4. I have heard and observed these ceremonies with various tribal elders throughout my life.

> though a part of me has been left behind in those Osage hills. . . . We live in two worlds. In the Native American world, our relatives surround us. We are related to everything. We walk upon Grandmother Earth . . . and we address the sun as "Grandfather." We live where we bless ourselves every day. Where everything we do has a meaning. We listen to our elders and sing the old songs. Our ceremonies take place throughout the year. Everything we do begins with a prayer to the Creator. We are always on Indian time and there is plenty of good Indian food to eat.
>
> But we also have to exist in the non-Native world. A place where we have to dress a certain way, go by clock time, and always are serious at work. A place where money is all that counts along with how much we earn and how we earn it. . . . People appear to always be in a hurry. Everyone seems to be a stranger. They pray once a week while in church and they pretend to have no relatives.[5]

Writers call these differences by many names—e.g., urban, white, Anglo, modern—but the difference is palpable. Many other Native Americans feel this pull between cultures, myself included.

In Kluckhohn and Strodtbeck's classic Values Orientation study that came to be informally known as the Harvard Values Project, they evaluated five communities in the southwest for their values orientation along with variations within and outside the groups. Two of these groups included the Rim-Rock Navajo and the Zuni Indians. The study was helpful to my own doctoral research in identifying the basic values orientations that have come to be categorized under such terms as the "unconscious system of meaning," "core culture," or "cultural themes." Spradley and Rynkiewich add to my effort to define values and their relationship to worldview:

> Values are conceptions of what is desirable. As assumptions about what is and what ought to be they shape every aspect of people's lives . . . The sum total of a culture's values produces a particular worldview, a total framework which provides an integrated conception of reality.[6]

The result is that one cannot have a worldview of reality free of values. Everyone has a worldview and everyone has values that make up their worldview. We use these values to negotiate our lives. We have talked about how the Native American worldview is built around a spiritual concept of

---

5. Moore, *Genocide of the Mind*, 36.
6. Spradley and Rynkiewich, *Nacirema*, 361.

the Harmony Way or what some might call shalom. Later, I will address some of the many values associated with a Western worldview.

Within Native American religious concepts of reality there is a primal worldview of harmony related to God through creation, with an inseparable link among all living things. The Harmony Way worldview appears to lend itself to a set of commonly held values. The Christian faith offers similar values found with the idea of shalom. Our Native American spirituality is closely tied to the idea that creation is good and one way the Creator is revealed is through the creation. Within Christianity is found a similar idea closely linked to what people call natural revelation, which always points to God.

What I am proposing is that the Western, post-Enlightenment, modern worldview has actually moved people farther from the scriptural shalom reality taught by Jesus, and by doing so, often erased truly Christian values. I am suggesting that the path of recovering a vital Christian spirituality in America may be to understand shalom and its American Harmony Way corollary that resided in this country prior to European arrival.

Questions for Reflecting

1. Would you be comfortable substituting the word *healing* for *salvation*? Why or why not?
2. What does it mean to be "perfect" as "God is perfect"?
3. In what ways has your view of the Scriptures been challenged by reading this chapter?
4. How does the idea that Jesus had a more Indigenous and wholistic worldview than those moderns reading it from a post-Enlightenment worldview challenge your ways of thinking?

Chapter Nine

Shalom Values and the Humpty Dumpty Dilemma

> "For Christ himself has brought peace (shalom) to us."
> —Ephesians 2:14a (NLT)

The Ancient Israelite system of well-being, including governance, economics, and spirituality, from which Jesus descended, was steeped in what I refer to as the shalom-sabbath-Jubilee system. The system was holistic in scope and supported by the tithe, and by both implicit and explicit rules for sharing one's wealth. God's people were to abide by laws that set aside a portion of their wealth for the poor and disenfranchised, as well as tithe into the system that supports the laws. Explicitly, rules of governance such as the tithe, setting aside a portion of one's land, and leaving the edges of one's fields for gleaning were firmly set. At the same time, there were implicit injunctions to go beyond the prescribed safety net set by the laws. People were expected to be generous beyond the law when it came to the whole community of creation. Consider the following.

Deuteronomy 24:19 (NLT)

> When you are harvesting your crops and forget to bring in a bundle of grain from your field, don't go back to get it. Leave it for the foreigners, orphans, and widows. Then the Lord your God will bless you in all you do.

Deuteronomy 24:20 (NLT)

> When you beat the olives from your olive trees, don't go over the boughs twice. Leave the remaining olives for the foreigners, orphans, and widows.

Deuteronomy 24:21 (NLT)

> When you gather the grapes in your vineyard, don't glean the vines after they are picked. Leave the remaining grapes for the foreigners, orphans, and widows.

The shalom-sabbath-Jubilee system was set up to ensure both regulatory function and suppleness of conscience. These were not just moral laws and decisions of private generosity, they were necessary to create a just system. The old argument by conservatives in the US that one cannot legislate morality does not hold water in God's shalom-sabbath-Jubilee system. While it would be easy for persons under such systems to simply obey the rules and feel like they had done their moral duty by fulfilling the letter of the law, pressure was applied through other channels to go beyond the rules of sharing into personal acts of generosity and kindness. It took both civil laws and personal generosity to create a balanced system. The rules guided one to do the right thing but the personal admonitions challenged one to move beyond the letter of the law by transforming one's heart and imitating the example God sets for all to observe.

> The transformational aspects of shalom are apparent in the divine model. In scripture, God is active through creation, in personal relationships, in covenant relationships, in the incarnation of Jesus, and in redemption; consequently, shalom is reflected in all God's activity. Shalom, therefore, is not detached from the reality of everyday life in the world nor is it in any sense super-spiritual, utopian or otherworldly; rather, it exemplifies how seriously God takes the world.[1]

The emphasis here on one's personal transformation concerns action, the very practical aspects of the value of living out shalom in everyday life. Active and practical, shalom does not avoid the realities of an imperfect

---

1. Woodley, *Shalom and the Community of Creation*, 22.

world but moves in a persistent confrontation with those values that encourage one to hoard and be miserly. The model for such a system is Creator God.

We are to cooperate by sharing natural resources rather than hoard them for personal pleasure or profit. Access to water, food, housing, clean air, and all natural resources should consider equality and equity before the severe restraints of privatization occurs, not after. In ancient Israel these safety nets ensured everyone had something, and were a balance of what we dub today as socialistic and capitalistic systems. Yes, people owned private land, but one-seventh of each person's land was also required to be set aside annually for the poor and for the wild animals to enjoy. The safety net of always leaving portions of land fallow to be shared was a socialistic system of equity, ensuring everyone had something. Jubilee, which occurred every fifty years, required all land to go back to the original owners, all slaves to be set free, and all debts to be forgiven. This action prevented any one person or one family from becoming too wealthy or too poor. In this sense, the great leveling effect ensured a system of equality—a very limited form of capitalism.

The apostle Paul's admonition in 1 Corinthians 8:11B–15 (NLT) speaks of the kind of equity in ancient Israel and that Jesus taught when he said we should love our neighbors as we love ourselves. There seems to be little space between systemic ethical guidelines and personal guidelines. Those conservative arguments about "if God's people just took care of the poor the government wouldn't have to" are entrapped in superficial categories. In God's purview, the right thing to do is always right, whether by government decree or individual conscience.

> Give in proportion to what you have. Whatever you give is acceptable if you give it eagerly. And give according to what you have, not what you don't have. Of course, I don't mean your giving should make life easy for others and hard for yourselves. I only mean that there should be some equality. Right now you have plenty and can help those who are in need. Later, they will have plenty and can share with you when you need it. In this way, things will be equal. As the Scriptures say, "Those who gathered a lot had nothing left over, and those who gathered only a little had enough."

So, what causes captivated the Western worldview to regard private ownership and capitalism as superior to a system of equality and equity, full of legal safety nets and personal generosity? While economic theory and history are beyond the scope of this book, I would like to suggest there were some metaphysical ideas that influenced Western society, especially as we now face such extremes in the realms of poverty, child hunger, the housing crisis, the medical insurance crisis, war, and ecological devastation. The worldly philosophies of the Greco-Roman world created unnatural space between humans and the Creator, between humans and other humans, between humans and the rest of creation, and turned what is natural into a mechanistic, individualistic, and capitalistic worldview.

Making Dualism Whole

As I mentioned earlier, I consider Plato, a student of Socrates, to be the father of our most insidious form of the modern dualism that persistently plagues our society at every level. What level of dualistic tendencies Plato glean from Socrates, we may never know. Most of what we know about Socrates is found in Plato's writings. Because of Plato's literary style, likely influenced by his former profession as a playwright, it is often difficult to understand, with the characters represented in his two semi-fictional writings, *The Republic* and *Apology*, which thoughts should be attributed to Plato and which thoughts actually belong to Socrates.

Regardless, the basis of what we call Platonic dualism is the emphasis on the ethereal, abstract part of reality over and above the material, concrete part of reality. In a Platonic dualist understanding, the material world is a shadow or an illusion and one's reality is wrought through reason and the imagination. The idea of a thing, in Platonic dualism, exists independently in time and space, representing the good and perfect world, while physical manifestations are merely imperfect shadows, copies of the ideal. In other words, the abstract idea of something is more real than the concrete thing itself.

In his time, Plato established what was perhaps the first school of philosophy, the Academy. His founding of the Academy was in major juxtaposition to existing schools, which trained people in the practical skills of various professions. If one wanted to become a politician or an architect or a builder, one received tutelage from someone in that particular profession. Plato's school was not about the practical but about thinking. It held a value that taught students that thinking well about life should be of more importance than a life lived. Plato's understanding of the importance of thought was quite innovative and perhaps a needed balance to the humdrum life of the everyday worker. Had it not been for one of his students, Aristotle, Plato's work would likely not have been as consequential at it ended up being.

Aristotle became one of the most influential philosophers and scientist in the Western world until the modern era. Although Aristotle did not fully agree with his teacher's understanding of metaphysics, the die was already cast. Once one's reality has shifted from the influence of dualism (and the influence on Aristotle was caught as much as taught simply by studying in a school of philosophy), all things in one's world become hierarchical and of either greater or lesser importance. Besides being an astute philosopher, Aristotle was also a scientist, creating something like what we know today as "the scientific method." He observed life around him and classified it according to his observations. These superficial classifications and categories included people. Some people, according to Aristotle, were naturally made to be slaves, and others rulers. Of course, people in his own class status were consider to be rulers, but according to Aristotle, through education, people in a slave status could potentially rise above their natural state. Later, Aristotle's theory of the natural slavability of those considered to be inferior was picked up and commodified by the sixteenth-century Spanish theologian Sepulveda, who defended Spain's right to enslave and colonize the Indigenous people of the West Indies.

While it is difficult to put all the blame for modern slavery on Aristotle, the rationale loosed into the world for creating such superficial categories has been used to justify all sorts of evil, including modern West African chattel slavery, and in particular, white supremacy. How did these two Greek philosophers amass so much influence in today's world? Really there were two factors that spread the presumed gospel of Greek influence around the world and posited it in our modern era. The first was via a student of Aristotle. While traveling, Aristotle was asked by King Philip of Macedonia to become a teacher for his son Alexander. The influence that Alexander the Great had on spreading his teacher's esteem for Hellenism around the world was unparalleled. The second influence, the Renaissance, was a result of a somewhat nostalgic recall of the glory days of Greco-Roman society, which especially took Western Europe by storm between the fourteenth and seventeenth centuries.

The Renaissance (or "rebirth") saw the revitalization of Greek culture and thinking. The influence of Greek art, architecture, law, literature, and so on was uncanny. Western Europe took on the unifying influence of what it considered to be the crux of higher civilization by imitating the ancient Greeks and reviving the "classics" of literature handed down from Greece and Rome, including the philosophies of Plato and Aristotle. Two particularly influential movements were born during the Renaissance period that would affect Christianity, largely, by then, Western European in scope and influence. These influences were the Reformation/Counter-Reformation and the Enlightenment.

The Protestant Reformation occurred in the sixteenth century and affected not only religion in Western Europe, but politics, philosophy, and culture. As the modern nation-state emerged in Europe, religion became infused with politics in a way different from the former Constantinian empire-driven marriage of Christianity and politics via hierarchical dictates. After the Reformation, each individual adopted the offspring of the new religious fervor excited by various nation-states. Christianity and Christian nationalism became a "natural" belief from which it would never recover. Various kings and other rulers set the tone for either religious tolerance or persecution and those of minority religions and movements became the victims, and later often the perpetrators of religious persecution. In the Reformation era, and the reaction to it by the Roman Catholic Church, the Counter-Reformation, the people made the new civil religions their own. The ubiquitous influences of Greek philosophical ideas, given new life in the Renaissance, continued to weave themselves into various theologies and political ideas upheld by the nation-states, to the point where one's religion could easily be identified by their nation.

During the Enlightenment period, or age of reason, considered to be of most influence in the seventeenth century, philosophers and scholars, who often spoke for and to religion, arose in a way not seen since the Greco-Roman period. The influence of the dualistic thinking of Enlightenment philosophers was obvious as seen through leading figures such as Descartes, Kant, Bacon, Schleiermacher, Smith, and others. Ironically, many of the theorists of the Enlightenment are considered to be both theologians and "natural philosophers." My argument is that dualism and its progenies of hierarchy, superficial categorization, individualism, privatization, anthropocentrism, and other influences are quite unnatural and contradict a whole view of reality and what is naturally given as a gift by God.

The earth and the heavens or any other dimensions are all working together to make one whole reality I call the community of creation. The community of creation involves all seen and unseen aspects of our world.

What one part does affects all the others. Humans are not above nature but simply a part of the whole community of creation. There is no hierarchy but rather there is a system in which we all cooperate and participate. There is, in reality, no such thing as a bipartite (body and soul) or tripartite (body, soul, and spirit) human being. All parts equal a whole, including intuition, extrasensory perception, ancient memory, and more. All of these things together make us human.

In a dualistic worldview our thoughts, philosophies, and theologies become disembodied. Dualism especially causes religious people to believe that their God is at work uniquely in their religion more than God is at work in the world, even though most believe their God created the world. This often has led to their inactivity in the "outside" world through complacency brought on by our own religious pride. Dualism causes us to neglect the truth found in most religions: that God is at work in the whole world. Physical/mental or physical/spiritual dualism results in there being no certainty of one whole reality but rather living into the parts as if they were the whole, not seeing the humanity or the needs outside our own bubbles, creating blindness to the needs of those outside our own group, or even outside our own individual selves.

Making People and Creation One

Anthropocentrism is a word we use to describe a view of humanity over nature as masters, sometimes called stewards. Much of this theology has been developed from the early Genesis story and the command for humans is to "rule over and subdue the earth." But I would argue that in the Genesis story human beings are created last, not to "rule," but to fill the need to co-sustain the earth; not last as the "crown of glory," but as the only creatures uniquely equipped to co-sustain the rest of creation. Responsibility, not privilege, is the key to understanding the story. Our call is not to rule over the land but to serve and preserve *God's* creation in a way that produces abundance. To be a co-sustainer in the community of creation is foundationally what it means to be human and made in God's image.

> Immediately after the creation of 'Adam, Creator gives the man and woman stewardship over the garden where they have been placed. Humanity will partner with Creator in creation care so that the world "is fruitful and multiplies" (1:28). Emphasis is often placed on the first two verbs (1:28) used to describe human

responsibility for creation, "subdue" (*kabash* . . .) and "have dominion" (*radah* . . .). But the last two verbs used in these texts (2:15) illuminate humanity's unique stewardship responsibility. The man and woman are commanded "to work, to serve, to till" (*abad* . . .). Stewardship means that humans are to *work with* the earth so that every aspect of the physical creation in all its resplendent diversity will prosper. They are also told "to watch, to guard, to preserve" (*shamar* . . .) God's good creation (2:15). Stewardship means that humanity hovers over the creation like parents watch over, guard, and protect their newborn child. In God's image, as humanity watches over and works with the diverse creation it will produce abundant and flourishing life for each and every element and creature. Violation or abuse of this *shalom stewardship* ultimately will threaten all creation.[2]

While Terry McGonigal uses the term *stewardship*, I prefer co-sustain, which I feel reveals a level of activity and a partnership between Creator, humans, and the whole community of creation. The clear admonition from God is to care for the whole community of creation as spelled out to Israel in numerous Scripture passages such as Leviticus 25:1–7 (NLT):

> While Moses was on Mount Sinai, the Lord said to him, "Give the following instructions to the people of Israel. When you have entered the land I am giving you, the land itself must observe a Sabbath rest before the Lord every seventh year. For six years you may plant your fields and prune your vineyards and harvest your crops, but during the seventh year the land must have a Sabbath year of complete rest. It is the Lord's Sabbath. Do not plant your fields or prune your vineyards during that year. And don't store away the crops that grow on their own or gather the grapes from your unpruned vines. The land must have a year of complete rest. But you may eat whatever the land produces on its own during its Sabbath. This applies to you, your male and female servants, your hired workers, and the temporary residents who live with you. Your livestock and the wild animals in your land will also be allowed to eat what the land produces.

Notice in this passage that the wildlife is taken care of, as well as allowing the land to rest. God's concern is for the whole community of creation and for concern over the land itself, not just for the well-being of people. The tithe was also to care for the neediest in society, as we see in Deuteronomy 14:28–29:

2. McGonigal, "If You Only Knew What Would Bring Peace," 4.

> At the end of every third year, bring the entire tithe of that year's harvest and store it in the nearest town. Give it to the Levites, who will receive no allotment of land among you, as well as to the foreigners living among you, the orphans, and the widows in your towns, so they can eat and be satisfied. Then the Lord your God will bless you in all your work.

The whole of shalom-sabbath-Jubilee was set up as a system that allowed the land, the people, domestic animals, and wildlife to co-exist in harmony. If humans were tempted to begin to understand themselves as superior to any other class of people, to any form of wildlife or any domestic animals, or even the land itself, they were reminded through their laws that they are simply a part of the whole community of creation and their role was to be caretakers or co-sustainers of the whole community of creation, not lords over everything else.

Anthropocentrism, borrowing thought from compartmentalization, dualism, and hierarchy, allows classification of humanity outside of the created order to the point where human beings are seen as existing over, and apart from, creation. A Western anthropocentric view understands humans as having the right of supreme rule over all creation, to the point where all creation is subject to humanity. Anthropocentrism allows human beings to view the resources of the world as commodities made for their pleasure or for extraction, without thought of the whole of the ecosystemic reality. An anthropocentric worldview misses the intimate relationship humanity shares with all Creation in the web of life. In the words I have heard from Indigenous activist and planter Winona LaDuke, "Regardless of whether or not they have roots or fins or legs or wings, they are all our relatives."

Making Many Categories One Reality

One of the marks of colonial power is to name or rename everything, especially naming things after so-called discoverers or conquerors. In empire the "winners" can be constantly reminded, and remind those they conquered, who is in power. Around my region, Wy'est became Mount Hood, Nch'i-Wana became the Columbia River, and of course, Turtle Island became America, all reminders to everyone of who "owns" the land and by proxy, who owns the people within those lands.

Another aspect of the obsession with naming everything is creating superficial categories that explain or re-explain the world in the terms of the colonizer. I say "re-explain" because, ironically, many of our original Indigenous names simply explain what something does or its specific characteristics. Wy'est (Mount Hood) is the "big mountain." Nch'i-Wana (Columbia River) is the "big river." Turtle Island, as we saw earlier, has a whole story that explains its name, shape, and purpose. While breaking down the form and function of any given thing can provide helpful information, it is easy to concentrate on a particular area or category and forget that the category itself does not function alone.

Take for example the medical field. Specializations such as cardiology, obstetrics, and neurology are specific categories that specialize in an area of a person's health. Yet, if any one of these categories fails to work from the perspective of the whole health of a person, any number of things can go wrong. We see many people die because of complications from prescription drugs from various specialists that negatively interact with one another. On a whole other level, how many medical specialists consider the diet of a person when treating a specific area they consider to be unrelated to diet? How many consider the relational stress of the person? How about what the person has been dreaming about? We are not even just a whole body but there is much more to us beyond our physical selves. Superficial categorization can be very helpful at times, but we must constantly remind ourselves that we are much more than our parts and each affects the other in a whole.

Making Abstraction into Reality

For the most part, the modern, industrialized, mechanistic Western worldview begins with the abstract. Like moving toward the vortex of a tornado, it focuses its lenses into ever smaller, extrinsic categories, hoping for what will result in a particular practice. Rarely, though, does that alignment of "first think, then do" result in a consistent praxis. One need only consider the history of the Western church to realize the inconstancy in this way of thinking. Indigenous worldviews often begin with the practical, and, like a pebble in a pond, the practice finds its way into ever-widening circles of application. I always say, "one good question can lead to worlds of discovery" but sometimes we should even hold our questions.

When tutored by Indigenous elders in several ceremonies I noticed a pattern of observing with all your senses, practice, receive correction, think and pray about it, practice more, receive more correction, continue to think and pray about it. Understand the system you are a part of, for example, and how the same principles apply to other areas of life, then continue to practice and after years of practice and thinking, and applying to other areas, while still learning, always learning, you may be ready to teach others. I once asked a question early on of an elder instructing me in a ceremony. He didn't answer me. Hours later he said, "You know that question you asked me? How much did you pray about that before asking me?" Sometimes even questions should be kept to oneself. The process is more important than the answers. In the Western mind all things are possible in the abstract. In some ways this imaginary is a gift to be embraced and used for important discovery. At the same time, the abstract realm of the Western mind can easily become unmoored by depersonalizing one's imagination to reality in pursuit of the ideal.

Sometime around the 1970s in America people become overly concerned about their own bodies. That's when fashion became such a leading industry, as did various forms of diets, the rise of plastic surgeries, and the health food revolution. This era also suffered an onslaught of anorexia and bulimia. Perfectly healthy people, mostly young women, thought of themselves as being too fat, even though they were not. Some suffered to the point of starvation, and tragically, some to the point of death. Society had planted the seeds of an image of a perfect body in their minds to the point that they could never be satisfied with their own bodies, regardless of how much weight they lost, in the minds of the victims of these maladies. In reality, it was not their bodies that needed correction but their minds. The two could not come into one whole reality.

Anorexia and bulimia are examples of disembodied thought: the reality of a person's body is substituted for the image one sees in their mind when one suffers from such a malady. Poor theologies, and resultant poor missiologies, are also examples of disembodiment and the basis for people's split understanding of reality. The work of Friedrich Schleiermacher at the University of Berlin influenced American theology and the American church by dividing reality between the practical and theoretical. The problem in such a sharp divide of reality is that these false dichotomies, when believed, take on a whole life of their own and create their own momentum. The divide, especially noted in academia, found the Western world living into the superficial categories of reality that it had created. Textual studies, history, and theology were separated from practical areas, that is, practical theology, and in hierarchical rank, the practical theology was in the lower realm. Western Christians, formerly established in an essentially holistic religion, found themselves developing and perfecting a worldview possessed of a divided reality that stressed the theoretical over the practical.

Christian mission, prior to the Enlightenment, was considered the "mother of theology,"[3] but after the influence of the Enlightenment period, what Christians believed and what they actually did could be rationally understood separate from each other. In other words, rationalization created space for one to hold correct doctrinal beliefs (orthodoxy) and not practice them. In a Western Enlightenment-bound worldview, categorically ordered and hierarchically seated, it was possible for a person, church, or denomination to justify their Christian faith even though their actions were deemed contrary to Christianity, as long as they held the correct doctrine. Epistemologically, the correct rationale now equalled truth.

Making Individual into Corporate

The Scriptures were not written for me, they were written for us. In such an individualistic society as ours, it is hard to wrap our heads around a salvation beyond a single individual, one at a time. But the Scriptures were not written by people with such a mindset. They were written by people who understood the value of the group. The benefit to an individual came as a result of the benefit to the group. Most of the time when Paul writes "you," it should rightly be translated plural as "you all." He is most often addressing the whole community. The difference is clear: an individualistic worldview and theology says "we are because I am," whereas a more community-based worldview and theology says, "I am because we are." While in America we teach community-based values when kids are younger in such areas as team sports, when we become adults, as we are preparing for SATs and careers, we are taught to becomes less cooperative with others, more competitive, and it's every person for themselves.

A capitalistic economic system based on an individualistic worldview is perhaps the opposite of what is taught in the Scriptures. Shalom-Sabbath-Jubilee–based laws created room for individuals to become wealthy for a time being, until Jubilee, the great equalizer was enacted every fifty years. Until that time, each person's wealth was used to create foundational safety nets for those less wealthy and even for strangers needing help. Salvation or better said, healing, should be thought of in a similar way. Healing can come to a community through the influence of shared values and laws

---

3. Bosch, *Transforming Mission*, 489.

based on these values. An individual reaps the benefits of this community healing and may personalize it as their own. Such healing can come from the community to the individual or from the individual to the community; either way, the process of healing is occurring.

When Jesus shared the good news, it was never meant to be exclusively for individuals, but for both the community and the individual, each influencing the other. Think of how the Philippian jailer's whole family was healed. In a community-oriented worldview, the whole system is affected, not just the individual. In each of Jesus' parables of the Lost Sheep, the Lost Coin, and the Lost Sons, what do they do when they find healing? They share it with their community and celebrate! Shalom love is contagious and meant to be shared, not "hidden under a bushel." Community is meant to be taken seriously even if it grates against our own American value of individualism.

We hear of mission efforts that report "whole tribes being saved." Why? Because in a community, what is good news for the individual is good news for everyone in the community. In community-based theologies, it would be selfish for one to hide one's wealth from the rest of the group. Wealth, freedom, new ways of thinking about the world, discovery, and so on are meant to be shared with others with whom we have a connection. Unfortunately, the connection in modern, individualistic society is lost, and what we call mission becomes a chore rather than a natural outflow of personal and structured love.

Making Hierarchy into Egalitarianism

Platonic dualism forces or presupposes a hierarchical worldview. When life is viewed through a dualistic lens that presupposes the ethereal reality to be more real or superior to the material reality, the equality of any two aspects of reality is impossible.

In a hierarchical worldview everything is juxtaposed and rated more than or less than, which leaves little space to hold two seemingly unrelated aspects of reality in tension and equally important. It naturally follows in a distorted hierarchical worldview that humans are greater than anything else in the community of creation, men are greater than women, whites are greater than BIPOC or foreigners, straight is greater than queer, and the list goes on. On such false premises theologies have been made, laws have been enacted, wars have been started, and so many innocent lives have been degraded, humiliated, treated unjustly, and lost.

Jesus certainly taught against hierarchy. Jesus taught equality. In Matthew 20:24–26 (NLT) Jesus' words stand in contrast to the Romans who had a strict hierarchy and were the colonizing and occupying force of that day. Jesus said, "You know that the rulers in this world lord it over their people, and officials flaunt their authority over those under them. But among you it will be different. Whoever wants to be a leader among you must be your servant." This passage has been sermonized and theologized and treated as a goal of Christian virtue, but the inescapable fact remains that the Roman Gentiles had a strict hierarchy and Jesus was saying those who follow him needed to enact the opposite.

The church, under Greek influence even in the first century, may have adopted hierarchical standards inadvertently at first. Edward Schillebeeckx, in his book *The Church with a Human Face*, points out that the original Jesus movement was egalitarian and most likely similar in form to a loose congregationalism governed (at least by 100 AD or so) by egalitarian groups but never without leadership—originally apostolic and later connected by evangelists and prophets—and always organized at some level.

Schillebeeckx points out that by 100–120 AD, Ignatius of Antioch had contextualized church structure around the military organization of imperial Roman-occupied lands that organized administration around dioceses and parishes—with the bishop equaling the field general. But in Alexandria, clear up until the early third century, the church was ruled by co-equal boards (a council of elders as well as a council of youngers) in a generally democratic format—so there were actually at least two completely different forms of organization. It was under Cyprian (late 300s) that the church took its more or less Western form that has been accepted as the norm in Western Christianity. Like so many other forms of contextualization, it was their idea of contextualization in their own context, but they normalized and universalized their context to fit the whole world. Also notice that what later became titles holding demonstrable authority like *episcopoi* and *presbyteroi* were likely better understood as functional titles in the early church.[4]

When the Roman emperor Constantine subsumed Western Christianity in the fourth century, the church had already provided the rationale and the theologies needed for him and his theologians to enshrine

---

4. This recap was taken from a footnote in my book *Decolonizing Evangelicalism*.

hierarchy into Christianity for millennia to come. Christianity has never recovered from the marriage of the church and state, nor from its hierarchical governance. But these were not the teachings of Jesus.

Making the Past into the Present

A society's view of time orientation affects everything. One of the ways to spot how deeply one is entrenched in a Western worldview is in one's use of time. North American Indigenous people call the use of time "Indian time" and Western folks call yours "normal," but we call it "white man time." An Indigenous understanding is built on story and the primacy of relationships, while white man time is built upon minutes and hours being saved or spent.

Although most Indigenous peoples are now steeped in modernity, there is still a negligible difference in what modernity demands of us and alternate views of time such as "Indian time," or "African time," or Filipino time." Think of short-term mission trips overseas and how the Americans' view of time is much more succinct and demanding. Time orientation is a difficult concept to visualize, but when one runs their life according to a clock it is easy to segment time into concrete meaning. It is more difficult to talk about time orientation as an abstract reality.[5]

The main difference in time orientation between Western and non-Western views concerns present engagement above future scheduling. In 1917, venerated Keetoowah medicine man Redbird Smith spoke of his understanding of religion and the present in this way:

> This religion as revealed to me is larger than any man. It is beyond man's understanding. It shall prevail after I am gone. It is growth like the child—growth eternal. This religion does not teach me to concern myself of the life that shall be after this, but it does teach

---

5. My time orientation categories themselves were developed primarily using Kluckhohn and Strodtbeck's Values Project literature, although it did occur in the earlier literature studies as: "an orientation to the past which honors tradition, and to the present in taking life as it comes" (Kelley, "Traditional Native American Values") and "Orientation to the present. Being, rather than becoming" (Evergreen State College, "Traditional Native American Values"). The Values Project considered past, present, and future orientations but they admitted that time orientation was difficult to test (which gives some credence to my stated concern). Kluckhohn and Strodtbeck perhaps summarized it best by stating that a past and present time orientation is "a source of knowledge and continuity that keeps the Present stable and the Future predictable" (*Variations*, 325) and that among the Indigenous people tested, "time was not viewed as a commodity."

> me to be concerned with what my everyday life should be. The Fires kept burning are merely emblematic of the greater fire, the greater Light, the Great Spirit. I realize now as never before it is not only for the Cherokee but for all mankind.[6]

In Smith's view, the present is where his spirituality exists. He has little concern for the future. This value of past and present cosmic orientation can be reduced to a micro level to help us understand how Native American life is lived on a daily basis. I have heard Native Americans say of people who operate within the confines of the dominant culture, "they have a clock inside their head," meaning they live their life in relation to a tighter time schedule than do Indians. In order to understand the natural rhythm of traditional Indians, especially those living in traditional communities on the reservations, the tighter time schedule must become less rigid.

Native Americans generally do not adjust well to the dominant cultures' value of time. While it may seem like a good use of time to people from Western cultures to mark the hours and even the minutes, Native Americans and many other non-Western cultures lean more toward valuing the organic interactions of place and people. The idea of *place* is related to creation-based spirituality. The Kantian philosophical divide concerning the concepts of *time* and *space* were ideally a balance of Western and non-Western thought. Yet, the West historically placed the emphasis on *time*, to the deprecation of serious thinking concerning *space* (or what I prefer to call *place*). When thinking about a creation-based spirituality, *place* takes on relational aspects that may be neglected by an emphasis on time.

Time tends to be event-oriented in nature. Americans have adopted a "temporal materialism" that lends itself to events. As mentioned earlier, the importance of these events becomes a *pseudo-place* for Westerners, from which they draw their identity. Event-oriented people seem to adapt easily to changes in locale. The new generations of event-oriented people are able to pass down the myth of *pseudo-place*, whereas land-based, *place*-oriented peoples seem to be more bound to a *place* as a base of identity. When place-oriented people are removed from their place, such as when Native Americans were removed from their homelands, they have great difficulty. Often, such differing views of time means that people end up talking right past each other, as noted in the following quote.

> When the domestic ideology is divided according to American Indian and Western European immigrant, however, the

---

6. Young, *Quest for Harmony*, 149.

> fundamental difference is one of great philosophical importance. American Indians hold their lands—place—as having the highest possible meaning, and all their statements are made with this reference point in mind.... When one group [American Indian] is concerned with the philosophical problem of space and the other [Western European immigrant] with the philosophical problem of time, the statements of either group do not make much sense when transferred from one context to the other without proper consideration of what is happening.[7]

The two different understandings concerning time about which Vine Deloria speaks is important if we are to understand how "Indian time" is a value that goes far beyond just being late for a meeting. Deloria believed that place-oriented peoples are concerned with truth in their own context, whereas time-oriented people tend to make truth abstract and apply it to any situation at any time.

> American Indians and other tribal peoples did not take this path in interpreting revelations and religious experiences. The structure of their religious traditions is taken directly from the world around them, from their relationships with other forms of life. Context is therefore all-important for both practice and the understanding of reality. The places where revelations were experienced were remembered and set aside as locations where, through rituals and ceremonials, the people could once again communicate with the spirits. Thousands of years of occupancy on their lands taught tribal peoples the sacred landscapes for which they were responsible and gradually the structure of ceremonial reality became clear. It was not what people believed to be true that was important but what they experienced as true. Hence revelation was seen as a continuous process of adjustment to the natural surroundings and not as a specific message valid for all times and places.[8]

A temporal worldview has limitations. It must have a real beginning and a real end. Spatially oriented worldviews have no need to inject this extreme view of historic and future reality upon themselves or others. With Native Americans the value of the now is the critical moment. The future has not happened. This is easily illustrated in ideas concerning "Indian time." As I stated earlier, philosophical constructs concerning time are difficult to discuss, but Indian time is a stark difference in reality compared to Western

---

7. Deloria and Wildcat, *Power and Place*, 143.
8. Deloria, *God Is Red*, 65–66.

clock time. What Indian time means practically is that our events and appointments will begin when everyone eventually shows up, despite any plans to have folks there at a certain time reflected by the clock. Indian time is regulated by place and experience, not by a clock.

Also, among Indigenous peoples the future is determined by looking to the past. Native Americans depend upon our stories, ceremonies, and traditions to guide us to a good future. Often that future is best expressed through exploring things from the past. We mine our past and those gems are our payment to the future. That is why our stories and other past concerns are so very important. Without our past, we cannot be a people of the future. My Mi'kmaq friend Terry LeBlanc tells the story of his grandfather taking him deep into the woods when he was younger. His grandfather told him to look twice as much at the scenery behind him as he moved forward, because if he did not recognize where he had been, he would never find his way out of the woods. This story has become a metaphor for Terry as he speaks on this subject.

There is also a fluidity between past and present. When sharing, Native American elders often drift freely between current and past events. They may begin a story by saying it began a long time ago but it is likely that the behavior or problem they wish to address is occurring in the present. As stated before, concerning our learning through reflected experience, we learn about how to live now through examining what has happened in our history.

Additionally, our present reality affects future generations. Indigenous peoples view the importance of the past to be critical in the way we live the present, so we can project what might be our better future. It is not as though Native Americans don't consider the future. One study from Evergreen State College in Washington suggested that there is an ethos among Native Americans that all things will eventually unfold in their time. As I understand it, this is not a causal statement but rather one that reveals the primacy of living in the moment. In the same way that there is a relationship between Native American views of the past and the present, there is a relationship between the present and the future. A common adage heard around Indian country is, "What we do today will impact the next seven generations." This is a widely held warning among Native Americans when considering the relationship of our present decisions to how they will affect those in the future.

Shalom Values and the Humpty Dumpty Dilemma

Making the Propositional into Story

In the popular movie *Smoke Signals* (now a somewhat famous Hollywood Indian film because it was the first to be written, directed, produced, and acted primarily by Indians), Victor, the young Indian protagonist, is trying to convince his mother that he will keep his word. He asks her if she wants him to sign a paper and she replies, "No way! You know how Indians feel about signing papers!" The fact that Native Americans mistrust the words of treaties (and well we should after so many treaties with the United States have been broken) has as much to do with the form of a written document as anything. The broken treaties only serve to substantiate the mistrust in all nonpersonal communicative forms. I have heard elders say, "I don't like talking on the phone because I can't see the person's heart who I'm talking to." There is a general mistrust among Indigenous people, especially traditional people, of any form of communication except oral, face-to-face encounters. This made alternative methods very difficult for many Native Americans during the COVID pandemic. The feeling is that there is primordial power in words spoken face-to-face in oral traditions. Because words are sacred, they are powerful entities and should never be misused or used deceptively. I think the same applies to other Indigenous people I have met throughout the years.

As a pastor I encountered this concern over orality in the form of understanding the Bible. If I read from the Scriptures the people did not seem to respond. If I paraphrased them, they listened more attentively. Some of the traditional people in the congregation expressed their thoughts when I asked them about what I observed. They said to me, "If we hear it from your heart we will believe you but we know that the white man translated the Bible and he could have removed things he didn't want us to hear or added things that are not true." Truth, to the traditional people in my congregation, was about hearing the words from a person's heart.

By the same token, those same people did not really care for what could be called "expository preaching." They felt the more my words had to be explained, the less power they contained. Our Native American values teach us that each moment is sacred and organic, and when one tries to record those sacred moments outside of the sacred space from which they came, it could be viewed as presumptuous. Our Indian people tend to feel that life should be taken as it comes, with each moment given its due when it occurs. Trying to recreate a sacred moment by recording it tends to stifle a mutual sense of trust among some Native Americans. What is sacred cannot be duplicated, nor can it be judged by the community. By that I mean, in Indian country a person must make himself or herself vulnerable in order to be heard. A person's words, along with their heart, will be judged at that time by the community. If the community who witnessed those words is absent later when they are examined by others it would be considered out of context. Words taken out of context are not important because they don't impart the same understanding they did when they were given. Understanding is sacred to the experience at the time and organic.

There is a space in traditional cultures for sacred historic and mythical stories and figures that is different than it is for the people of the West. Often, our Native American stories begin with a council of animals getting together to discuss something of importance. As I have shared stories with white children at times, they have interrupted, saying, "animals can't talk." Whereas Indigenous children first want to know what the animals had to say.

In the West there is a line of demarcation drawn between what is a fable and what is historic. Mythical figures like Paul Bunyan and Johnny Appleseed, although they may be based on historic figures, are told in an atmosphere of fairy tale or they mark the beginning of the story, "Once upon a time." Indigenous children hear stories of White Otter or the Peacemaker, and they are listening in a different way. What is true is different than what is fact. Truth in story comes from the story and storyteller, not historic fact, for Indigenous people. This is more akin to the type of thinking in the Bible when stories were told as well. Because there are often stories, ceremonies, and mnemonic objects that accompany Indigenous traditions, including places, natural features like the Sun, moon, and stars, and species of animals, trees, and insects, they have remained fairly stable. The continued passing of the oral history seems to help to ensure a return to or maintenance of the Harmony Way or shalom.

Questions for Reflecting

1. As you consider the whole of the ancient shalom-sabbath-Jubilee system, talk about the differences between social and personal equality and equity.
2. What are some ways we might work on our worldview to make it more wholistic? What are some of the areas in our personal lives, and

Shalom Values and the Humpty Dumpty Dilemma

the life of our churches, that need to become more wholistic? How do we get there?

3. In what ways can there be hierarchy with anarchy and order in chaos?
4. Is there a way story can be incorporated more into your worship service? How would that change things?

Chapter Ten

The Mission of Jesus

"Every teacher of religious law who becomes a disciple in the kingdom of heaven is like a homeowner who brings from his storeroom new gems of truth as well as old."—JESUS

WHAT IS THE GOSPEL (good news)? I was taught the core of the gospel is a set of beliefs that we share with others. Jesus was born, lived and died for us, and then resurrected to empower us, and if we believe in him, we will one day enter eternal life. While the content of this story is partially true, the premise is not. The core of the good news of Jesus Christ is not a message that one needs to simply believe, but rather it is a way in which life is lived out. To believe the gospel is not simply cognitive, but to believe the gospel is to live our lives in the same way Jesus lived his life. It is convenient that a society influenced so greatly by Platonic dualism could wrangle such a powerful witness, with such amazing implications, down to a set of propositions that tell us when we share the message, we are sharing the gospel.[1]

Jesus' life was lived as a mission for which he incarnated, lived, died, and resurrected! Our message, the message of the disciples, the message of the church, is not at all simply about what we say or what we say we believe

---

1. This is partially the fault of the timing of the European Reformation and Counter-Reformation, which occurs during the European Renaissance and what would become the European Enlightenment, drawing water from Greek thinking, including Platonic dualism and the individualistic influence of the Enlightenment. The over-influence of a person's individual faith and one's cognitive beliefs over experience was, in most cases, inevitable.

about Jesus, but the gospel is found in the power of what we do in Christ. After all, now that we all live in a world full of facts at our fingertips, knowledge is no longer power, if it ever was, but rather the power of the gospel is demonstrated through our doing the very same type of things Jesus did—those acts, based on values, for which he lived and died. So, it behooves us to ask ourselves, what was Jesus' mission based upon? Whatever the answer to that question, answers the question, "What is the gospel?"

There are many places where Jesus speaks explicitly of his mission and purpose, such as: to fulfill the law (Matt 5:17), to seek and save the lost (Luke 19:10), to destroy the work of evil (Mark 1:24), to heal (Mark 9:25), to call people to repentance (Luke 5:32), to do what the Father is doing (John 5:19), and the like. There are his many implicit missional actions, like lifting up the place of women (Luke 7:36–50), creating justice in local systems (Luke 19:8), creating equality (Matt 20:24–26), generating equity (Matt 19:21), and including non-Jews (John 4:20–26). All of these examples and more exhibit the values of the ancient system of what I call the shalom-sabbath-Jubilee principles. Certainly, above all else, as Jesus first announces his mission in what is his inaugural address, his coming out, his exposing himself to his hometown at the synagogue in Nazareth, is perhaps the most revealing of all other explicit or implicit missional proclamations. If we are to understand how Jesus understood himself, and his own life's mission, Jesus' words at Nazareth must be taken most seriously. In Luke 4:16–30 Jesus explains his purpose and mission clearly, linking the Jewish practices of the shalom-sabbath-Jubilee principle to his current mission, the same mission that all his followers are called to continue.

The Gospel of Shalom-Sabbath-Jubilee

Jesus is relying on ancient Judaism's understanding of shalom-sabbath-Jubilee constructs, which was informed by his understandings of the First Testament. But Jesus also understands the way of shalom differently than many others, as apparent in his interactions recorded in Luke. Many of us know the story but it is important to read it again before discussing it.

> Then Jesus returned to Galilee, filled with the Holy Spirit's power. Reports about him spread quickly through the whole region. He taught regularly in their synagogues and was praised by everyone. When he came to the village of Nazareth, his boyhood home, he went as usual to the synagogue on the Sabbath and stood up to

Mission and the Cultural Other

> read the Scriptures. The scroll of Isaiah the prophet was handed to him. He unrolled the scroll and found the place where this was written:
>
> "The Spirit of the Lord is upon me,
>   for he has anointed me to bring Good News to the poor.
> He has sent me to proclaim that captives will be released,
>   that the blind will see,
> that the oppressed will be set free,
>   and that the time of the Lord's favor has come."
>
> He rolled up the scroll, handed it back to the attendant, and sat down. All eyes in the synagogue looked at him intently. Then he began to speak to them. "The Scripture you've just heard has been fulfilled this very day!" Everyone spoke well of him and was amazed by the gracious words that came from his lips. "How can this be?" they asked. "Isn't this Joseph's son?" Then he said, "You will undoubtedly quote me this proverb: 'Physician, heal yourself'—meaning, 'Do miracles here in your hometown like those you did in Capernaum.' But I tell you the truth, no prophet is accepted in his own hometown. Certainly, there were many needy widows in Israel in Elijah's time, when the heavens were closed for three and a half years, and a severe famine devastated the land. Yet Elijah was not sent to any of them. He was sent instead to a foreigner—a widow of Zarephath in the land of Sidon. And many in Israel had leprosy in the time of the prophet Elisha, but the only one healed was Naaman, a Syrian." When they heard this, the people in the synagogue were furious. Jumping up, they mobbed him and forced him to the edge of the hill on which the town was built. They intended to push him over the cliff, but he passed right through the crowd and went on his way. (Luke 4:16–30)

Perhaps the best way to understand Jesus' missional announcement here is to take one section at a time. First, his initial announcement:

> The scroll of Isaiah the prophet was handed to him. He unrolled the scroll and found the place where this was written:
>
> "The Spirit of the Lord is upon me,
>   for he has anointed me to bring Good News to the poor.
> He has sent me to proclaim that captives will be released,
>   that the blind will see,
> that the oppressed will be set free,
>   and that the time of the Lord's favor has come."

The Mission of Jesus

> He rolled up the scroll, handed it back to the attendant, and sat down. All eyes in the synagogue looked at him intently. Then he began to speak to them. "The Scripture you've just heard has been fulfilled this very day!"

Jesus was reading that day from Isaiah 61. It might help to give some context. Israel in Jesus' day was waiting for a Messiah who would end the Roman occupation, declare Jubilee, and reinstate their former glory to them. Isaiah, writing much earlier, projects what that might look like when he states the words Jesus repeats. Much of Isaiah's words in the surrounding chapters appear to be a promise to Israel of a restoration of Jubilee or the Great Day of the Lord. Apparently, Jesus read only the parts of Isaiah he wanted them to hear that day. Clearly the people in the crowd had an idea of the promise to end the Roman oppression and reinstating Jubilee. So, what is Jubilee?

As mentioned earlier, Jubilee is connected to ancient Israel's sabbath system. There were sabbath days where Israel was told by God to rest on the seventh day. The land in this agrarian society was also subject to sabbath laws. One-seventh of each person's land was to be set aside and left fallow each year. In addition, every seventh year the farmer's whole property was to be set aside and left fallow. Why? The land that was left fallow was to be used by those who had no way of owning land and providing for themselves, which included priests, the poor—emphasizing widows, orphans, and immigrants—and for animal life, including both feral and domestic. At the conclusion of each set of seven sabbaths, there was a Jubilee year to be declared!

Before we seek to understand Jubilee, let's stop to consider what a society based on these sabbath laws looks like and what this has to do with Jesus. Every year every farm in this society had one-seventh of their land open for those (human and nonhuman) in need. At the same time some farms were on their sabbath year leaving their whole property as a food supply for the welfare of those in need. In addition, Israel was told not to glean the edges of their fields when they harvested, not to go back for a forgotten bushel of wheat of grapes, but to also leave those for the poor and disenfranchised. In such a society sabbath was the way in which those outside the system of privilege could glean and gather their own food with dignity. Systemically, it was a society of abundance and equity for all, with each having the ability to make themselves a living regardless of whether or not they owned property.

Jubilee, a part of the genius of the sabbath system, is the final goal of sabbath. Not only does Jesus identify himself as Jubilee, but sabbath is intimately linked to Jesus' identity. Jesus is called Lord of the Sabbath (Mark 2:28). He is our sabbath rest (Heb 3–4). Because the writers of Scripture are so willing to reveal Jesus as the preexistent Christ who undergirds the efficacy of creation itself (John 1:1–4, 10–14; Col 1:15–20; 1 Cor 8:6; Heb 1:1–2), we are forced to wrap our heads around the notion that it was actually Jesus the preexistent Christ who created the world and everything in it in six days (as the story goes). It was then Jesus, the preexistent Christ, who rested on the seventh day, the sabbath. In other words, Jesus Christ, who created the world also incarnated in it to reconcile the world and all creation to God and the whole community of creation. And how do we connect Jesus to Jubilee, besides his own missional identification?

On the fiftieth year, the year of Jubilee, there was major redistribution of wealth and spreading of justice. In the Jubilee year all debts were canceled. That's right, tear up your mortgage and cut up your credit cards, because there was no longer any debt. In addition, all land was returned to the original owners! Wow! Every Native American's dream! Those who had bought land within that half century had to give it back to those who had sold or lost land, so they had their land returned. A restoration of Jubilee meant that for just over two generations, no family could get too rich and no family could get too poor. This system equalized everyone just to start again. It was a do-over, a combination of what moderns could refer to as limited capitalism and socialism.

Of course, while Jubilee was good news for some, it was bad news for others, as noted in Mary, Jesus' mother's song found in Luke 1:46–55. Mary was told she would bring the Messiah into the world and understanding what that meant, she sang a song consisting of these lyrics:

> Oh, how my soul praises the Lord.
> How my spirit rejoices in God my Savior!
> For he took notice of his lowly servant girl,
> and from now on all generations will call me blessed.
>
> For the Mighty One is holy,
> and he has done great things for me.
> He shows mercy from generation to generation
> to all who fear him.
> His mighty arm has done tremendous things!
> He has scattered the proud and haughty ones.
> He has brought down princes from their thrones

The Mission of Jesus

> and exalted the humble.
> He has filled the hungry with good things
> and sent the rich away with empty hands.
> He has helped his servant Israel
> and remembered to be merciful.
> For he made this promise to our ancestors,
> to Abraham and his children forever.

Notice, the poor in this scenario make out much better than the rich. As the Jewish Messiah, Jesus himself, in the fulfillment of Jubilee, is becoming the great equalizer. Jubilee means restored justice to the oppressed and to prisoners. In Jubilee all prisoners are to be released, having their sentences commuted, all oppressed are to be set free from their oppressors, and those who are blind will once again see.[2] Jesus is clear in his message that he is claiming to be "the one" who will change things forever and that change meant justice for all. If Jesus had decided to keep reading the Isaiah scroll that day, it would have been clearer to the listeners, perhaps, the reason this great societal shift must occur. In Isaiah 61:8 it reads, "for I, the Lord, love justice!" Sabbath and its Jubilee fulfillment were necessary to ensure everyone had a fair shake, that everyone got a shot at justice. It may have been delayed, but one day, people knew, justice was finally coming around! As Martin Luther King Jr. reportedly said, "The moral arc of the universe is long, but it bends towards justice."

It is clear that Jesus inhabits and personifies sabbath and its fulfilment in Jubilee. But the core value upon which sabbath is based is shalom. To observe sabbath is not just to observe a sabbath day, sabbath land management, a Sabbath year, and Jubilee. Sabbath is indivisible from the whole construct of shalom. Remember the reason all the fields are left fallow and not gleaned completely? Feeding the poor, needy, disenfranchised, and wildlife—that is all about shalom. Do you recall the justice, equity, and principles of equality that exist in Jubilee? Again, they are part and parcel of shalom. There is so much to say about shalom, perhaps the grandest theological construct in Scripture, so much that I wrote a whole book about it and still could not cover all its aspects.[3]

---

2. There is often a discussion surrounding this passage of whether or not "blind eyes opened" is metaphorical or literal. We do have instances of Jesus giving physical sight to the blind, but perhaps both apply. Can it not be both?

3. See Woodley, *Shalom and the Community of Creation*. Also see Brueggemann, *Peace*.

Mission and the Cultural Other

While I cannot write another book solely about the construct of shalom in this space, let me recap and summarize by saying shalom, and its related derivative words, represents the balance and harmony we find in the Genesis creation story, and the image of the prophets who call Israel to make and keep peace, act justly, do mercy, and walk humbly with God. Shalom is a society that resolves conflicts without war, and where justice, equality, and equity are the standards, where everyone is fed when they are hungry. Shalom is more than peace. Shalom is a society filled with diversity but free of hurtful divisions and factions. Shalom is the goal of the church and the kingdom of which Jesus spoke. Shalom is extreme hospitality and all the values found in love. In fact, shalom is structured love.

How do we know we are in the realm of shalom? We know by how we treat the most marginalized and disenfranchised in society, including the non-human community of creation and the earth itself. If they are well taken care of, shalom is possible. If not, there can be no shalom until everyone has enough of whatever is needed. Broken shalom is laid out in the first eleven chapters of Genesis, where shalom is fractured at almost every level. Shalom can be broken between humans and God, between families, and in society itself. Poor treatment of the earth is broken shalom. Mistreating the widows, orphans, and immigrants is broken shalom. Abandoning the poor and needy, the most marginalized in society, is broken shalom. Put simply, sin is the absence of shalom. While shalom is the larger construct, it makes it easier to remind ourselves of its practicality when I refer to it as shalom-sabbath-Jubilee. Jesus fulfills all these with his incarnation, life, ministry, death, and resurrection. He is our shalom (Eph 2:19).

As I stated earlier, Jesus understood the ancient shalom-sabbath-Jubilee construct differently than many others. He came to earth to energize that construct, to fulfill it, to make it his mission and ours. How is that done? Let's take a look at the second half of the story in Luke:

> "Certainly, there were many needy widows in Israel in Elijah's time, when the heavens were closed for three and a half years, and a severe famine devastated the land. Yet Elijah was not sent to any of them. He was sent instead to a foreigner—a widow of Zarephath in the land of Sidon. And many in Israel had leprosy in the time of the prophet Elisha, but the only one healed was Naaman, a Syrian." When they heard this, the people in the synagogue were furious. Jumping up, they mobbed him and forced him to the edge of the hill on which the town was built. They intended to push him over

the cliff, but he passed right through the crowd and went on his way.

Here, Jesus points out the difference in their understandings of shalom. He tells how God sent one of his greatest prophets to help feed a poor widow (who is clearly not Jewish). Then he speaks of another great prophet who assisted in the healing of a Syrian oppressor (a foreigner). His hometown crowd is not happy with his interpretation. They preferred to be thought of as God's "darlings," God's chosen people. While it's true that God does have favorites, it is also true that we are all God's favorites, as Jesus must have read in so many passages, including Amos 9:7:

> "Are not you Israelites
> the same to me as the Cushites?"
> declares the Lord.
> "Did I not bring Israel up from Egypt,
> the Philistines from Caphtor
> and the Arameans from Kir?"

I must admit I've never seen a bumper sticker reading, "God loves the Philistines" or "Arameans, God's People of the Covenant." And notice, Jesus is adamant about making his point because he points out the historical facts that there were many hungry widows in Israel and many lepers too! To the Nazareth crowd Jesus was saying, "God was slumming with you people's enemies, and God liked it!" Jesus kind of rubs their noses in it to make a point, then, oops! The point was taken too sharply and they tried to kill him by throwing him off the cliff. Chalk it up to message not well received.

Remember the ever-present holy triad that points to whether or not a community has shalom—widows, orphans, foreigners/immigrants? In Jesus' story, the Syrophoenician lady was the widow. Naaman the Syrian was the foreigner. I asked myself if the crowd at Nazareth was already tracking with where Jesus was headed. But where, or maybe better asked, who, was the orphan who completes the holy triad? The orphan, who was being made as he told the story, who was the guy being cut off, disinherited, orphaned from his hometown, was Jesus himself. May we receive his mission better than his earliest neighbors did.

Questions for Reflecting

1. Define the essence of the gospel.

2. What questions do you still have concerning the shalom-sabbath-Jubilee construct?
3. Explain the mission of Jesus.
4. How might you and your church practice shalom among yourselves and in your community?

Conclusion: Ending at the Beginning

A Letter of Confession

A FRIEND OF MINE was struggling with his privilege as a white male in a racist, white supremacist society. Scott wrote me this letter, not long before he passed from this world with brain cancer. With his permission to share "in any way you see fit," I offer an excerpt.

> What's a White guy to do? My dad was a racist. He never sat me down and instructed me on the fine points to White superiority, but I certainly picked it up. Dad intentionally made sure I knew how to milk the cow, drive the tractor, and shoot clay pigeons, but he never actually taught me to hate or disdain people on the basis of cultural or physical attributes. Nor did I inherit it in my Norwegian/German genes. Rather, I acquired it by listening to the way adults acted and talked. Racism—in my case, anyway—wasn't taught, but caught.

I always appreciate hearing my friend's thoughts about his own struggle because it reminds me that the Way is hard. I don't think the way forward is complicated, but it is difficult to face, especially if we hold privilege others don't. Especially when society has been structured to accommodate and promote white people, mostly middle- and upper-class males, and to keep the cultural other held back. Especially when the church and missional enterprise has been so soaked in it that they don't even recognize that racism and privilege are the waters the American missional movement was born and continues to swim in. What's the church to do? What's the denomination to do? How do we move forward from here?

When I share with groups of well-intentioned white church folks about the reality of the past that they somehow knew, and yet couldn't admit, invariably the first question I get is, "How do we fix this?" I'm used to the question so I don't get offended by it, but it is loaded with bad assumptions. It assumes the problem can be fixed. It assumes the same white savior complex that has driven missions up to this point, that if given the chance, "We can fix it." The question assumes that the cultural other is not powerful enough to fix their own problems. It assumes that white folks are still in power. And, maybe, it assumes that it can be fixed without deep sacrifice.

Words. Western society, in their Platonic dualism has developed the right words for every situation. But what do the words mean? Most often, not much. Action is required, but for people to act, they must have the right attitude. I like words that mean something. Please hear the words of my Cayuga friend as he speaks to white missionaries in the most moving and honest address I think I have ever heard:

> I have been to the halls of power. There is nothing for me there. I've been to the hallowed headquarters where everyone speaks in whispers, afraid of disturbing the powers-that-be. I've walked on your marble floors and upon your Persian rugs. I've sat in your great big leather thrones, where you decided the fate of all the little people, all those you needed to pay your bills. I've stood by your fountains springing up to impress me just how special you are. I've listened to your spin and the tales of win/win—all so much honey covered hemlock.
>
> I don't want your expertise. I don't want your wisdom. I don't want your competence. I don't want your money. I don't want your pity. I don't want your sweat and advice. I don't want you to reach down to me. I don't want you to look down on me. I don't want your perfect image. I don't want your unsullied testimony. I don't want your perfection.
>
> I want your heart. I want your failures. I want your humility. I want to see you for who you are, not for who you think I need. I want you: good, bad and ugly. I know you are going to hurt me. Don't hold back on me just because of this. I know you are ashamed of yourself. So am I. That is why we have a Saviour. That is why we are brothers. That is why we are family. We are peers. You are not my Great White Father. You are my Lost White Brother. I have something to say to you. I have information that you need. I have gifts that will make you complete, just like it is with you. I need you. I need what you have to offer. I need the gifts our Creator put into you.

Conclusion: Ending at the Beginning

Just don't Lord it over me. I am your peer. I am your peer without a PhD. I am your peer without an education. I am your peer without money. I am your peer without my land. I am your peer without political power. I am your peer without numbers. I am your peer with all my loss. I am your peer with all my pain. I am your peer with all my failures. I am your peer even though I don't think like you. I am your peer even if I use a different part of my brain. I am your peer even if you don't respect me. I am your peer even if I make you uncomfortable. I am your peer even if you cannot hear what I am saying. I am your peer even if someone else seems more important than me, more important to you.

You are my peer even if you are culturally autistic and will never be able to read the cues I give you, even when I spell it out to you as clear as I can. I am your peer and I deserve your ear. I am your peer and I deserve your heart. I am your peer and I will continue to patiently wait for you to get it, to finally read my social cues, to stop violating my dignity and not even see what you are doing. One day you will get it. One day you will read my social cues. You will see the tear in my eye before it falls. You will hear the ache of my heart before you understand. You will listen to my story until you are reduced to a puddle of tears. You will stay there until God resurrects you. One day you will find yourself standing up and you will look to your right and you will see me. You will look to your left and you will see me. You will be holding my hands and finally we will be one brotherhood, one family under God. Not with you as my superior. Not with you as my father, for there is but one Father. You will finally be my brother.

We are the conscience of your technology. We are the humanizers of your institutions. We matter, quite apart from your recognition of our worth. We are the sacred clowns to level dignity. We are the beloved community of Martin Luther King Jr.'s dream. We are a threat to entrenched powers-that-be who refuse to open the doors of opportunity and choice to all. We are a challenge to the mindset of greed, the avarice of Babylon, calling for the equitable distribution of resources in the spirit of the Jewish Year of Jubilee. We are good medicine for you.[1]

Perhaps the worst assumption of all held captive in the question, "how do we fix it?," is the assumption that the oppressors understand the problem, or that they can even relate to it. While it is true that an outsider may never really understand the problem, they still must listen. Then listen some more.

---

1. Jacobs, "Mitigating Missionary Autism."

Then continue listening until they realize they can't really understand the complex issues of being the cultural other in a white supremacist society, and still, it breaks their heart. At some point, the question will come up again but it will be spoken closer to something like, "Besides continuing to listen, please let me know when you think there is anything you want me to do." After listening has stewed for a long, long time, doing will be the key. But as a junior partner, not a senior partner. And, perhaps, given the right attitude and time passed, perhaps a co-partner.

And, for that reason, this is not a "how-to" book on mission. That book may well come soon enough, but this is a book about listening, and repenting, and learning a new way to think about ourselves and mission among the cultural other. We end at the beginning.

Narrative Bibliography

THERE ARE MANY GREAT resources for study. As a professor, I have come across so much in my lifetime, each piece adding perspective to the big picture and each adding understanding for that time. There are, however, five books that stand out related to this particular journey, five books that I consider essential to the process of decentering white supremacy in mission. None of them are about mission. But within these books you will find the history behind many of the conclusions I draw in this book about mission. I suggest reading them in the following order:

The History of White People by Nell Irvin Painter. Dr. Painter is African American, the Edwards Professor of American History emerita at Princeton University at the time of this writing. Painter's book begins in antiquity and especially helps us to understand how the category of the *cultural other* surfaces, in what she explains was, to the Greeks, the *exotic*, how those ideas first come into being among Greek society, and how the Greeks began to think of themselves as civilized and other societies as barbarians.

The Romans are the inheritors of Greek ideas of civilization and in the book *Savage Anxieties: The Invention of Western Civilization*, Robert A. Williams Jr., award-winning author, legal scholar, and member of the Lumbee Indian Tribe shows how Roman civilization becomes the template for Western civilization. The Greeks had their barbarians and the Romans their savages.

Next, read *Stand Your Ground: Black Bodies and the Justice of God*. The Rev. Canon Kelly Brown Douglas is the canon theologian at the National Cathedral. In 2017, she was named dean of Episcopal Divinity School at Union Theological Seminary. As a Black womanist theologian, Brown excels in so much, but the jewel I appreciated most in this book was her understanding of the impact of Anglo-Saxonism, inherited from Rome in England, and the classification of the cultural other as the "heathen" traveling from empire to empire, and finally to American shores.

For the overall picture of the failures, complications, and remedies for Western society, read ***Utopian Legacies: A History of Conquest and Oppression in the Western World***, by John Mohawk. Mohawk adds a view of the grand narrative from a Native American prospective. John Mohawk was a professor at SUNY Buffalo, an internationally respected elder, a member of the Seneca Nation, and a farmer. His work has influenced me more than perhaps any other writer.

Finally, in my book ***Shalom and the Community of Creation: An Indigenous Vision***, I propose a model of American shalom for us all.

Other books by Randy S. Woodley

Indigenous Theology and the Western Worldview: A Decolonized Approach to Christian Doctrine. Grand Rapids: Baker Academic, 2022.

Becoming Rooted: One Hundred Days of Reconnecting with Sacred Earth. Minneapolis: Broadleaf, 2022.

Decolonizing Evangelicalism: An 11:59 p.m. Conversation. Co-authored with Bo C. Sanders. Eugene, OR: Wipf & Stock, 2020.

The Harmony Tree: A Story of Healing and Community. Illustrated by Ramone Romero. Victoria, BC: FriesenPress, 2016.

Shalom and the Community of Creation: An Indigenous Vision. Grand Rapids: Eerdmans, 2012.

"'The Harmony Way:' Integrating Indigenous Values Within Native North American Theology and Mission." PhD diss., George Fox University, 2010.

When Going to Church is Sin: And Other Essays on Native American Christian Mission. Scotland, PA: Healing the Land, 2007.

Living in Color: Embracing God's Passion for Ethnic Diversity. Downers Grove, IL: InterVarsity, 2004; Grand Rapids: Chosen, 2001.

Bibliography

Baker, Kevin. "'1491': Vanished Americans." *New York Times*, October 9, 2005. http://www.nytimes.com/2005/10/09/books/review/09baker.html?ex=1286510400&en=6c2b14837f45babb&ei=5090&partner=rssuserland&emc=rss.

Baldridge, William E. "Toward a Native American Theology." *American Baptist Quarterly* 8 (December 1989) 227–38.

Beaver, R. Pierce. *Introduction to Native American Church History*. Tempe, AZ: Cook Christian Training School, 1983.

Bevans, Stephen. *Models of Contextual Theology*. Maryknoll, NY: Orbis, 1992.

Bosch, David J. *Transforming Mission: Paradigm Shifts in Theology of Mission*. Maryknoll, NY: Orbis, 1991.

Brueggemann, Walter. *Peace*. St. Louis: Chalice, 2001.

Buxton, Ryan. "So You're About To Become A Minority . . ." HuffPost, April 20, 2015. https://www.huffpost.com/entry/so-youre-about-to-become-a-minority_n_553011f0e4b04ebb92325daf.

Churchill, Ward. *A Little Matter of Genocide: Holocaust and Denial in the Americas 1492 to the Present*. San Francisco: City Lights, 2001.

Comaroff, Jean, and John Comaroff. *Of Revelation and Revolution: Christianity, Colonialism, and Consciousness in South Africa*. Vol. 1. Chicago: University of Chicago Press, 1991.

Dear, John. *Peace Behind Bars: A Peacemaking Priest's Journal from Jail*. Kansas City, MO: Sheed and Ward, 1995.

Deloria, Vine, Jr. *God Is Red: An Indian View of Religion*. Golden, CO: Fulcrum, 2003.

Deloria, Vine, Jr., and Daniel R. Wildcat. *Power and Place: Indian Education in America*. Golden, CO: Fulcrum, 2001.

Demos, John. *The Heathen School: A Story of Hope and Betrayal in the Age of the Early Republic*. New York: Alfred A. Knopf, 2014.

Dobbs, Jack P. *Authority and the Early Quakers*. South Gloucestershire, UK: Martin Hartog, 2006.

Evergreen State College. "Traditional Native American Values and Behaviors." http://www.evergreen.edu/nwindian/curriculum/valuesbehaviors.html.

Freire, Paulo. *Pedagogy of the Oppressed*. New York: Continuum, 1992.

Gaustad, Edwin S. *A Documentary History of Religion in America: To the Civil War*. Grand Rapids: Eerdmans, 1982.

Gill, Jerry H. *Native American Worldviews: An Introduction*. Amherst, NY: Humanity, 2002.

BIBLIOGRAPHY

Ignatiev, Noel. *How the Irish Became White*. New York: Routledge, 2008.

Jacobs, Adrian. "Mitigating Missionary Autism." *NAIITS Journal* 9 (2011) 59–70.

Jenkins, Philip. *Dream Catchers: How Mainstream America Discovered Native Spirituality*. New York: Oxford University Press, 2005.

John Paul II (pope/saint). "Tribute to Father Junipero Serra and California's Missions." YouTube. https://www.youtube.com/watch?v=UrVppTbWKTg.

Josephy, Alvin M., Jr., ed. *The American Indian*. Introduction by John F. Kennedy. New York: Random House, 1963.

Kelley, Susan D. M. "Traditional Native American Values: Conflict or Concordance in Rehabilitation?" *The Journal of Rehabilitation*, April 1, 1992. http://www.encyclopedia.com/do/1G1-12874897.html.

Kipling, Rudyard. "The White Man's Burden: The United States & The Philippine Islands, 1899." In *Rudyard Kipling's Verse: Definitive Edition*. https://sourcebooks.fordham.edu/mod/kipling.asp.

Kluckhohn, Florence Rockwood, and Fred L. Strodtbeck. *Variations in Value Orientations*. Evanston, IL: Row, Peterson, 1961.

Lindquist, C. E. E. *New Trails for Old: A Handbook for Missionary Workers among the American Indians*. New York: National Council of Churches of Christ, 1951.

Mann, Charles C. *1491: New Revelations of the Americas before Columbus*. New York: Alfred A. Knopf, 2005.

McGonigal, Terry. "'If You Only Knew What Would Bring Peace': Shalom Theology as the Biblical Foundation for Diversity." Paper. https://citeseerx.ist.psu.edu/viewdoc/download?doi=10.1.1.486.658&rep=rep1&type=pdf.

McLoughlin, William G. *Champions of the Cherokees: Evan and John B. Jones*. Princeton: Princeton University Press, 1990.

Miller, F. T. "The Prophet and Tecumseh." http//courses.missouristate.edu/ftmiller/Documents/Prophet&Tecumseh.htm.

Moore, Mari Jo. *Genocide of the Mind: New Native American Writing*. New York: Thunder's Mouth/Nation, 2003.

Newton, Paula. "'Unthinkable' discovery in Canada as remains of 215 children found buried near residential school." CNN, June 1, 2021. https://www.cnn.com/2021/05/28/world/children-remains-discovered-canada-kamloops-school/index.html.

Niezen, Ronald. *Spirit Wars: Native North American Religions in the Age of Nation Building*. Berkeley: University of California Press, 2000.

Painter, Nell Irvin. *The History of White People*. New York: W. W. Norton & Company, 2011.

Pew Research Center. "America's Changing Religious Landscape." May 12, 2015. http://www.pewforum.org/2015/05/12/americas-changing-religious-landscape/.

———. "Modern Immigration Wave Brings 59 Million to U.S., Driving Population Growth and Change Through 2065." September 28, 2015. https://www.pewresearch.org/hispanic/2015/09/28/modern-immigration-wave-brings-59-million-to-u-s-driving-population-growth-and-change-through-2065/.

Rynkiewich, Michael, ed. *Land and Churches in Melanesia: Issues and Contexts*. Goroka, Papua New Guinea: Melanesian Institute, 2001.

Segal, Charles M., and David C. Stineback. *Puritans, Indians, and Manifest Destiny*. New York: G. P. Putnam's Sons, 1977.

Smith, Craig S. *Boundary Lines: The Issue of Christ, Indigenous Worship, and Native Culture*. Prince Albert, SK: Northern Canada Mission Distributors, 2001.

Bibliography

Snyder, Howard A. *Kingdom, Church, and World: Biblical Themes for Today.* Eugene, OR: Wipf and Stock, 1985.

Spradley, James P., and Michael A. Rynkiewich. *The Nacirema: Readings on American Culture.* Boston: Little, Brown, and Company, 1975.

Starkloff, Carl. *The People of the Center: American Indian Religion and Christianity.* New York: Seabury, 1974.

Sugirtharajah, R. S. *Asian Biblical Hermeneutics and Postcolonialism: Contesting the Interpretations.* Maryknoll, NY: Orbis, 2003.

———. *Postcolonial Reconfigurations: An Alternative Way of Reading the Bible and Doing Theology.* London: SCM, 2003.

Tinker, George E. *Missionary Conquest: The Gospel and Native American Cultural Genocide.* Minneapolis: Fortress, 1993.

Woodley, Randy S. "Indigenous Worldview as Original Instructions and a Critique of the Western Worldview." 2019 Hayward Lectures, October 21–23, Wolfville, NS, Canada.

———. "The Pope's Hypocritical Stance Towards Indigenous Americans Opens New Wounds: An Open Letter." *The Huffington Post,* September 27, 2016. https://www.huffpost.com/entry/pope-francis-native-americans-_b_8204896.

———. "Poverty and the Poor in North American Indigenous Traditions." In *Poverty and the Poor in the World's Religions: Religious Responses to the Problem of Poverty,* edited by William H. Brackney and Rupen Das, 378–410. Santa Barbara, CA: Praeger, 2019.

———. *Shalom and the Community of Creation: An Indigenous Vision.* Grand Rapids: Eerdmans, 2012.

Woodley, Randy S., and Bo C. Sanders. *Decolonizing Evangelicalism: An 11:59 p.m. Conversation.* Eugene, OR: Cascade, 2020.

Young, William A. *Quest for Harmony: Native American Spiritual Traditions.* Indianapolis: Hackett, 2002.

www.ingramcontent.com/pod-product-compliance
Lightning Source LLC
Chambersburg PA
CBHW022122160426
43197CB00009B/1126